# Upon this Rock
## (The History of FBC New Brockton)
## (1902-2023)

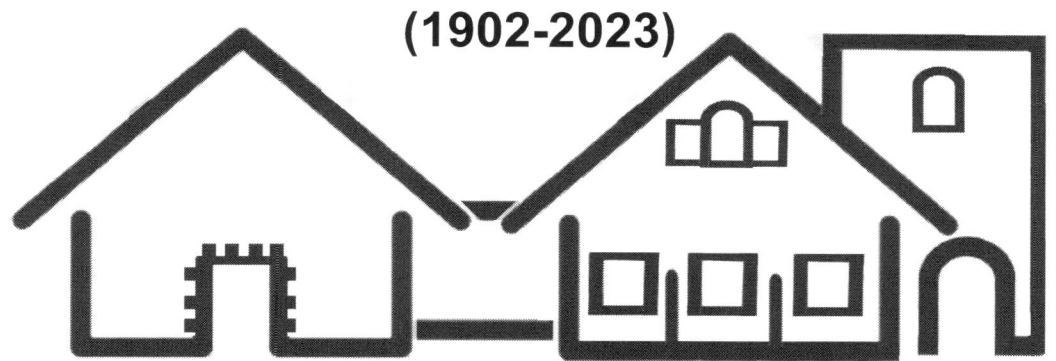

**Kyle St. Andrews**

# Table of Contents

**Dedication**
**Acknowledgement**
**Preface**
**Induction**
**Staff**

1. **The Roots** — 1
   Upon this Rock
   The Great Commission
2. **The Genesis of FBC New Brockton** — 3
   The Mysterious Man in the Long Coat
   The Revival that started it all
   The Establishment of the Church in Brockton
   The First Church Service
3. **The Church in its infant Age** — 7
   The First Pastor (Rev. Matthews)
   Getting involved in Community
   The First Church Building
   Rev. Hunter's Tenure
   The Year of Transformation (1907)
   Rev. Matthews second tenure
   The Men of the Church stepped up
4. **The Era of Growth** — 14
   Rev. Lee (1908-1909)
   Rev. Loftin (1909-1914)
   Rev. Pope L. Moseley (1914-1920)
   The Pastor Associational Years (1920-1924)
   Rev. Johnson (1924-1928)
   Rev. Bush (1929-1938)
   Re. Beasley (1938-1940)
5. **The Church's Golden Age** — 21
   The Debut of an Age (1940-1941)
   Rev. Fleming (1941-1944)
   Rev. Jones (1944-1946)
   Rev. Dykes (1947-1952)
6. **The Age of the Great Revivals** — 26
   Rev. Mezick First Tenure

    The Great Spiritual Awakening
    A Good Problem to Have
    Calling to the Ministry

7. **The Church's Silver Age**     36
    Entering the Silver Age
    The Return of Rev. Mezick
    Rev. Gales (1964-1966)
    Rev. McWhirter (1967-1969)
    Rev. Raley (1970-1972)
    Rev. Croft (1973-1974)
    End of an Age

8. **The Renovation Period**     44
    Rev. Henderson
    Renovation
    Rev. Barr (1993-1999)

9. **The Centennial Year**     49
    Y2K
    Centennial Celebration
    Rev. Hixson
    Rev. Stinson

10. **Dusk**     53
    Rev. Sims
    The Joint Revivals
    COVID
    The Twilight before the Dawn

11. **A Dawn of a New Dra**     58
    Rev. Pope
    Christmas Time
    A New Year
    Summer 2023

12. **The Pastors Vision**     65

13. **The Author's Commentary**     67

14. **FBC New Brockton**     70
    Deacons
    Men's Brotherhood
    FBC Bhoir
    The W.M.U.
    Sunday School
    Vacation Bible School

    Youth Group

    Men's Ministry

15. **The Gospel**     74

| | |
|---|---|
| **Recommending Reading** | 76 |
| **Appendix A** | 77 |
| **Appendix B** | 78 |
| **Appendix C** | 79 |
| **Appendix D** | 80 |
| **Appendix E** | 84 |
| **Appendix F** | 85 |
| **Appendix G** | 87 |
| **Appendix H** | 88 |
| **Notes and References** | 90 |
| **Index** | 105 |

# DEDICATION

To honor and pay tribute to the dedicated Brothers and Sisters who paved the way with their unwavering commitment to keep up the Good Fight and never waver from the mission. Additionally, we can not forget the individuals that were the visionaries who initiated, established, and tirelessly served this Church within this tight-knit community.

"Go ye into all the world, and preach the Gospel to every creature. He that believeth and is baptized shall be saved; but he that believeth not shall be damned." **Mark 16:15-16**

# Acknowledgement

This Project would not have been possible without the assistance of these following individuals:

The Pea River Historical Society

The Town of New Brockton (Mayor Kathy Holley & Chief Dale Grimes)

Coffee County Baptist Association (Ms. Emily Boykin)

The First Baptist Church of Enterprise (Ms. Rachel Pammer & Ms. Beth Smith)

The Alabama Baptist Missions (Mr. Micky Crawford)

The Alabama Baptist Historical Society (Mrs. Pat Mussel)

The Ladies of First Baptist of New Brockton (Mrs. Walker, Mrs. Campbell, Mrs. Reba)

The Enterprise State Community College Library

The Enterprise Public Library

The University of Chicago

The Troy University Library

The Samford University Library

The University of Alabama Library

The Auburn University Library.

First Baptist of Elba, Elba, AL (Mrs. Kathy)

Elba UMC

Alabama House (Capital)

Coffee County Courthouse

Bethany Baptist, New Brockton, AL (Rev. Grey Cotter)

Newton Baptist, Newton, AL

FBC Cairo, Cairo, GA

# PREFACE

This journey has been a wild and crazy ride. It all started with compiling information for the First Baptist Church of New Brockton's website. The more I dug into the history of the Church and the Community, the longer the rabbit trails got. My father (Leon Strickland) joined my journey through history, helping me compile information. It seemed like every time we got an answer to a question, a dozen more questions would appear. We came to the realization that we would have to unlearn what was taught us through traditions & folklore, and learn the truth of what really happened.

It was a never ending advantage to find and compile all the historical information. There was so much missing in the recorded history of the Church and the town, like street names being changed, maps of the whole Town of New Brockton being uncharted for decades and undocumented fires and floods destroying priceless information, leaving us digging deeper, trying to find any scrap of information with the hope that we could assemble them.

None of this would have been possible without the Historians and Authors that came before; Fred S. Watson, S. D. Fuller, Albert L. Strezier, Roy Shoffner, Amelia Herring Day, the journalist of The Enterprise Ledger, the Elba Clipper, The Dothan Eagle, and The Troy Messenger.

After all the endeavors to recount and find every single drop of the history of the First Baptist Church of New Brockton, you have to accept that some things are lost to history, because of fires, floods, storms, being left to the elements or sometimes just being mislabeled or thrown away.

What we did find was that First Baptist Church of New Brockton was not just some little brick church at the caution light in New Brockton, AL. It has a rich history and a beautiful story of how the town and outlying communities were blessed and flourished by the Men and Women of God from that Church. How they were part of creating and forming the Town of New Brockton and the outlying communities. The ideas, hopes, dreams and goals of the Church shaped and are still shaping the community today. The Church has never stopped its main mission to touch the community by sharing the Gospel of Christ Jesus. Which is that Christ died for our sins, was buried and rose again on the third day. That we are saved by Grace Alone, with Faith Alone, by Christ Alone.

It has been a pleasure meeting and getting to work with all the wonderful people of the Town of New Brockton and its outlying communities and First Baptist Church of New Brockton.

Kyle St. Andrews

September 10th, 2023

# Induction

The Baptist Faith came from the early 1600's when John Smyth removed himself from other Protestant denominations, the Anglicans, Lutherens, Presbyterians and Anabaptists in 1607 in Holland (Netherland). Smyth agreed with Ulrich Zwingli on rejecting paedobaptism (infant baptism). Believing in the Baptism of the Believer by immersion, the memorial of the Last Supper, opposed to consubstantiation and transubstantiation. The Baptist Faith originally was Puritans and Congregationalists. In 1612 Thomas Helwys founded the first Baptist church in England. The first Baptist church in America was founded in the 1630's by Roger Williams in Providence, Rhode Island.

The first Baptist Church in Alabama was Flint River Baptist Church, established on October 2nd, 1808. In a historical dispute within the Baptist faith that divided the Denomination in the early 1800s, which deeply divided the denomination. On one side, the Anti-Missionary Movement emerged to voice against the Educational and Mission societies that had been formed within some of the Baptist Associations. Their argument centered around the belief that since mission societies, Sunday Schools, and central church organizations were not mentioned in the New Testament. While on the other hand, the Missionary Movement supported the use of Educational and Mission Societies.

**Pastor** - Rev. Stephen Pope

**Youth Leader** - Jennifer Pope

**Music Director** - Chuck Nelson

**Church Clerk** - Janice Holloway
**Church Treasure** - Sharon Walker
**Nursery Coordinator** - Janice Holloway
**Usher Coordinator** - Noah Nolin
**Sunday School Director** - Kyle Strickland
**Sunday School Secretary** - Sandra Locklar
**VBS Director** - Danielle Donaldson
**Assistant VBS Director** - Sonja Steiner
**WMU President** - Midge Hogan

## Committees

**Hostess & Special Events** - Vicky Harrison, Wolf Steiner, Doris Nolin, Madelyn Adkison, Vicky Hollis

**Baptism** - Danielle Donaldson, Johnny Donaldson, Jean Doanldson

**Grounds** - Phil Freese, Vanessa Davis, Madelyn Adkison

**Properties** - Janice Holloway, Peggy Mixon, Dale Nolinm Chuck Nelson, Sharon Walker

**Music** - Jean Doaldson, Sonja Steiner, Chuck Hogan

**Budget & Finance** - Sharon Walker, Glenda Roberts, bonnie Campbell

**Decoration** - Rodger Harrison, Vicky Harrison, Chuck Hogan. Midge Hogan

**By-Laws & Constitution Revision** - Sharon Walker, Doug Nolin

**Benevolence** - Bonnie Campbell, Peggy Roberts, Faye Richardson

**Association Executive** - Chuck Nelson, Chuck Hogan

**Nominating** - Peggy Mixon, Glenda Roberts, Sonja Stiner, Chuck Nelson

**Sound Technician** - Kyle Strickland, Wolf Steiner, Noah Nolin

# Chapter 1

## The Roots

*"As ye have therefore received Christ Jesus the Lord, so walk ye in him: Rooted and built up in him, and stablished in the faith, as ye have been taught, abounding therein with thanksgiving."*
**The Epistle to the Colossians 2:6-7**

## Upon this Rock

On a calm spring day in the sacred Holy Land, JESUS found HIMSELF standing at the foothills of Mt. Hermon, along the coasts of Caesarea Philippi. HE turned to HIS disciple asking a question that still is echoed through history, "WHO do men say that I AM?"

The Disciple replied to their Rabbi, "Some claim YOU to be John the Baptist, others insist YOU are Elijah, and still, some say YOU are Jeremiah, or one of the prophets."

JESUS pressed them further, "But WHOM do you say that I AM?" Then Simon Peter, a simple fisherman who was one of the disciples, declared, "YOU are the CHRIST, the SON of the living GOD."

In that Divine moment, JESUS blessed HIS disciple by saying, "You are indeed blessed Simon, son of Jona, for this revelation has not been given to you by mere flesh and blood, but by MY FATHER WHO resides in Heaven, and I say to you, that you are Peter and upon this rock I will build MY Church and the gates of Hell will not prevail against it."

## The Great Commission

The author who accurately chronicled this account within the page of his Gospel also penned the profound words of CHRIST concluding the Gospel of Matthew, JESUS came addressing them, proclaiming, "All authority has been given to Me in Heaven and on Earth. Therefore, go forth and make disciples of all nations, baptizing them in the NAME of the FATHER, and of the SON, and of the HOLY GHOST:" This Divine mandate has resonated thought history, spanning from the Middle East to the corners of Europe, across the vast Atlantic Ocean to the newly found Americans, and ultimately found its way into the Southern State of Alabama, in a quaint little town called Brockton.

**Bible inside of the Church Tower Foyer**
**(Current)**

**Grand Piano in the Sanctuary**
**(Current)**

## Chapter 2

# The Genesis of a FBC New Brockton

*"Thy word is true from the beginning: and every one of thy righteous judgments endureth for ever"*
The Book of Psalms 119:160

### The Mysterious Man in the Long Coat

One day in early June in the year 1902 Rev. J. M. Moore, the pastor of Bethany Baptist Church and his son, Obe, had just returned home after a grueling long day in the field. As they were resting on their porch, while talking and gazing into the horizon, they saw a dark figure approaching. This mysterious gentleman, wearing a dark long frock-tailed coat and top hat, sporting a long mustache.

Rev. Moore made a remark, "Son, I've never seen that man before, but I'm sure he is a preacher." The dark figure came to the porch and introduced himself as Rev. Robert M. Hunter. He told them he had come for the purpose of trying to establish a Baptist Church in Brockton, because Brockton did not have a Church.

Brockton, a young community in the Wiregrass part of Alabama, had only recently been formed around Hugh Brock's little country store. The Townsfolk just had an election on May 31st of that year, to Incorporate the Town of Brockton as a Municipality. Rev. Robert M. Hunter, who just came from North Alabama from the Birmingham, where he was the Pastor of FBC Avondale (presently known as South Avondale Baptist) earlier that year, was a dedicated minister who had been traveling on train between the towns of Enterprise and Elba, the overseer and Pastor of both Baptist Churches; Enterprise Baptist (FBC

Enterprise) and Elba Baptist (FBC Elba). The void of a Church being in Brockton grieved him and he was moved by the Spirit to plant a Church.

## The Revival that started it all

On Monday June 30, 1902, a Revival Meeting unfolded in the Town of Brockton. This gathering took place beneath the open sky. It was known as a 'brush arbor' - a meeting place with tree branches and brush offering temporary shelter to protect them from the elements. Here, amidst the rustic beauty of nature, the Holy Spirit moved.

Twenty-one souls found Salvation, embracing Christ as their Lord and Savior during this profound revival. The townsfolk started talking about organizing a Baptist Church in Brockton.

## The Establishment of the Church in Brockton

On Thursday, July 10th, 1902, the birth of Brockton Baptist Church became a reality, and was constituted and established. With the guidance of Rev. Robert M. Hunter, and Rev J. M. Moore, as the Presbytery organizing the Church, Brockton Baptist Church was established. It was formed as a Missionary Baptist congregation, firmly distinguishing itself from the Primitive Baptist tradition.

The founding members, who laid the cornerstone of the faith in this community, included Mr. and Mrs. W. B. Harper, Mr. and Mrs. E. G. Brunson, Mr.

and Mrs. Dock Taylor, Rev. and Mrs. J. M. Moore, Miss Bertie Brunson, Miss Bessie Brunson, Miss Berchie McGee, Mrs. Malissa Marsh and Mr. Ed Brunson.[1]

These devoted individuals chose the meeting place for the newly organized Church in the Brockton School Building located on the south side of Massy Street (currently known as Lee St.) and the western side of Byrd's Mill Road (currently known as Church St.)[2].

This kind of school building is primarily designed for one or two classrooms. Recognizing the need for a dedicated place of worship, a committee was appointed with the task of building a suitable Sanctuary in the future.

The Church bore the name "Brockton Baptist", from the town it was founded in, Brockton. Which, in turn, owed its name to the esteemed town founder, Hugh Brock.

## First Church Service

On Sunday Morning, July 13, 1902, Brockton Baptist Church held its inaugural service within the walls of the Brockton School Building. This is where Rev. Robert M. Hunter concluded the revival meeting, attracting a great crowd that flocked to the Brockton School House to hear the Gospel preached.

At 9 a.m., a profound moment occurred as Rev. Robert M. Hunter administered the first baptism service for the people eager to join the Church. The waters of Byrd's Mill Pond were used to baptize Miss Mattie Wilson, Miss Josie Wilson, Miss Jessie Brock, Miss Ida McCree, Miss Florence Marsh, Miss Collie Brunson and Miss Pearl Dean as they publicly professed their faith in

---

[1] see Appendix B for Charter Member list
[2] see Appendix H for Map

CHRIST. At 11 a.m. everyone gathered back at the School House, because of a fall of a very fine rain, where Rev. Hunter preached his sermon.

**Rev. Robert Macon Hunter**
**(one of the Founding Presbytery)**

**The Old Brockton Wooden School Building**

**Home of Brockton Baptist 1902-1905**

(Artist Conception)

# Chapter 3

## The Church in its Infant Age

*"And Jesus saith unto them, Yea; have ye never read, Out of the mouth of babes and sucklings thou hast perfected praise?"*
**The Gospel according to Matthew 21:18**

## The First Pastor (Rev. Matthews)

Rev. Critten Livingston Matthews, the Pastor of Ozark Baptist (FBC Ozark) was called and assumed the mantle as the inaugural Pastor of Brockton Baptist in July 1902. Rev. Matthews, a Confederate Veteran, later came to know JESUS CHRIST as his LORD and SAVIOR in 1872. He was Licensed to Preach in the autumn of 1873 and initiated his ministry in Montgomery County, Texas, where he was Ordained there. In the 1880's, he came to the Great State of Alabama. He was renowned for baptizing over a thousand souls and played a pivotal role in establishing numerous churches. He was known as an Entrepreneur along with being a great Pastor, owning and operating a store in Ozark, Alabama.

During his first tenure at Brockton Baptist Church, Rev. Matthews also served many other churches as Head Pastor. He pastoried at Brockton Baptist, Bethel Baptist in Newton, Alabama, Damascus Baptists, and Indian Creek Baptist in Bullock Co., Alabama. Under his leadership, the Brockton Baptist Church made rapid progress and growth in the community.

## Getting involved in the Community

Brockton Baptist Church officially joined the Pea River Baptist Association in October 1902, marking a significant time in the historical growth of the Church. On a memorable Sunday, November 30, 1902, the Church welcomed Rev. Robert M. Hunter as Special Guest Evangelist.

However, in January 1904 brought challenges to Rev. Matthews was taken quite ill, grappling with symptoms that afflicted him for years to come. Despite his health struggles, in August of 1904, he preached a powerful revival at New Hope Baptist in Jack, Alabama, where 20 individuals were baptized.

During the very eventful year of 1904, Rev. Matthews served as pastor at Brockton Baptist, Indian Creek Baptist in Bullock Co, Alabama, Damascus Baptists, Victoria Baptist, and Inverness Baptist in Union Springs, Alabama.

In October of 1904, Brockton Baptist Church sent its first representatives to the Pea River Association meeting, which was hosted by Calvary Baptist Church in Enterprise, Alabama.

## The First Church Building

In the summer of 1905, the members of the Church continued to worship in the walls of the Brockton School Building until a plan to erect a Church Building took shape. The Building Committee, consisting of valued members of the Church including Mr. E. G. Brunson, Mr. W. B. Harper, Mr. Hugh Brock (the esteemed Founder of the Town of Brockton), Mr. J. P. Phillips, Rev. C. L. Matthews (who was serving as the Pastor of Brockton Baptist Church at that time).

The visionary Mr. Hugh Brock, the town founder, generously contributed the land which the Church would stand on. gave a lot for the Church to be built. This lot was located near the Atlantic Coast Line Depot, (which was near the washeteria from the 1950's) along the historic Byrd's Mill Road, which at that time was the public dirt road connecting Elba to Enterprise. This road is currently recognized as Church St. This plot of land is between Vester Cole St. and John St. on the southern side of Church St.[3]

The church building was completed at the cost of $90 for material, with volunteer labor of the Church Construction. The dedication service was conducted by Rev. C. L. Matthews. During this dedication service it was a special occasion. Winston W. Moore from Goodman, Alabama, was baptized and joined Brockton Baptist Church.

## Rev. Hunter's tenure

In the summer of 1905, Rev. Robert M. Hunter, the Minster that played a pivotal role in establishing the Brockton Baptist Church, returned to serve as Pastor. During his first year of tenure in 1905, he pastored at Elba Baptist (FBC Elba), Enterprise Baptist (FBC Enterprise), Damascus Baptist and Daleville Baptist. In the following year, 1906, The Ladies Aid Group, now known as W.M.U.(Women's Missionary Union) was formed. Since its inception in 1906, the W.M.U. has remained a cornerstone of the Church and a pillar of the Community. Mrs. Rosa B. Hunter, the Pastor's wife, was the first women's leader.

Furthermore, in that very same year of 1906, Mr. J. A. Wright, a devoted Deacon of the Church, took the lead in guiding the congregation toward progress

---

[3] see Appendix H for Map

to advance at its every opportunity. He was instrumental in aiding the Church to purchase its first musical instrument - a pump organ, purchased at the cost of $55. Notably, on Thanksgiving Day of 1906, the Merchants of The Town of Brockton unanimously closed their doors and gathered at Brockton Baptist Church to attend a sermon delivered by Rev. Robert M. Hunter.

**Pump Organ**

**(Artist Conception)**

## The Year of Transformation (1907)

On a Tuesday morning on January 22, 1907, disaster struck the Town of Brockton as fierce fire engulfed two businesses. Yet, just a few months later, on Monday, April 1st, 1907, Brockton underwent a significant transformation, officially changing its name to the "Town of New Brockton." The change was prompted by a perplexing mix-up within the U.S.. Postal Service, where mail intended for Brockton, Alabama often found its way to Blockton, Alabama. This change was duly recognized by both the Atlantic Coast Line and the U.S. Post Office.

Also, during this transformative year of 1907, the town's streets were not laid off then and being near the business section and the railroad, it was decided to move the Church Building was moved by rolling the Church building on Logs 400 feet to the east, on the southwestern corner of the intersection of Massy St. (currently known as Lee St.) and Byrd's Mill Road (currently known as Church St.).[4] During this time Brockton Baptist Church adopted the name New Brockton Baptist Church.

## Rev. Matthews second tenure

In December, 1907, Rev. C. L. Matthews, the inaugural Pastor of Brockton Baptist, resumed his duties as Pastor. During his second tenure, the Church's membership had grown to 98 members. Also, the Church property was valued at $500. In the summer of 1908 Rev. Matthews resigned as Pastor of New Brockton Baptist Church.

## The men of the Church stepped up

During the latter part of 1908, the Church was without a Pastor. On the week of October 19th to 21st, 1908, history was made as the inaugural Annual Session of the Coffee County Baptist Association convened at Calvary Baptist Church in Enterprise, Alabama. This was a consolidated session of the Pea River Baptist Association and Haw Ridge Baptist Association. New Brockton Baptist Church (being a member of the Pea River Baptist Association previously) joined Thirty-Two other Churches that comprised the membership of the Coffee County Baptist Association.

---

[4] see Appendix H for Map

New Brockton Baptist was without a Pastor during this time, but had messengers at this association meeting. They were Mr. R. Scheffer and Mr. E. D. Brooks. Also at this meeting, Four Missionary Societies were represented and recognized; New Brockton, Calvary, Enterprise and Elba.

**Rev. Robert Macon Hunter**

**(Brockton Baptist's 2nd Pastor 1905-1907)**

**First Church Building for Brockton Baptist 1905-1925**

**(Artist Conception)**

**Rev. Robert Macon Hunter & Mrs. Rosa B. Hunter**

**Rev. Dallas P. Lee**
**(New Brockton Baptist's 4th Pastor 1908-1909)**

# Chapter 4
## The Era of Growth

*"But his delight is in the law of the LORD; and in his law doth he meditate day and night. And he shall be like a tree planted by the rivers of water, that bringeth forth his fruit in his season; his leaf also shall not wither; and whatsoever he doeth shall prosper."*
**The Book of Psalms 1:2-3**

### Rev. Lee (1908-1909)

In November 1908, Rev. Dallas P. Lee, the former pastor of Blockton, Alabama was called by the New Brockton Baptist Church to serve as Pastor. Notably, during this period, he concurrently served as the Pastor of Elba Baptist (FBC Elba), Elba, Alabama.

During this time, Mr. J. A. Wright and Mr. John N. Wallace, dedicated Church Deacons, played a pivotal role in Church improvements, which included purchasing new pews to replace crude plank seats that had been used until that time. The cost of these improvements was $900.00, with a $100.00 down payment, with monthly payments set at $10.00.

After a year, in November 1909, Rev. Dallas P. Lee stepped down from his pastoral duties.

### Rev. Loftin (1909-1914)

In Late 1909, The Church sought and called Rev. J. M. Loftin, the former Pastor of Troy Baptist in Troy, Alabama to serve as Pastor.

A significant moment happened on October 29th to 31st, 1913 the 6th Annual Session of the Coffee County Baptist Association was held at New Brockton Baptist Church. This was the first time the Association met at New Brockton Baptist Church. The speakers were C. J. Bentley, and Dr. W. B. Crumpton, a Missionary of the Alabama Baptist.

## Rev. Pope L. Moseley (1914-1920)

In 1914, Rev. Pope Lloyd Moseley of Enterprise, Alabama answered the call of the Church to serve the role as Pastor. Rev. Moseley was known for his renowned sermons on the Baptism of the Holy Spirit, Repentance and Trust in God. October 23, 1919, Rev. P. L. Moseley delivered a powerful sermon at the 12th Annual Session of the Coffee County Baptist Association at Elba Baptist Church (FBC Elba) in Elba, Alabama.

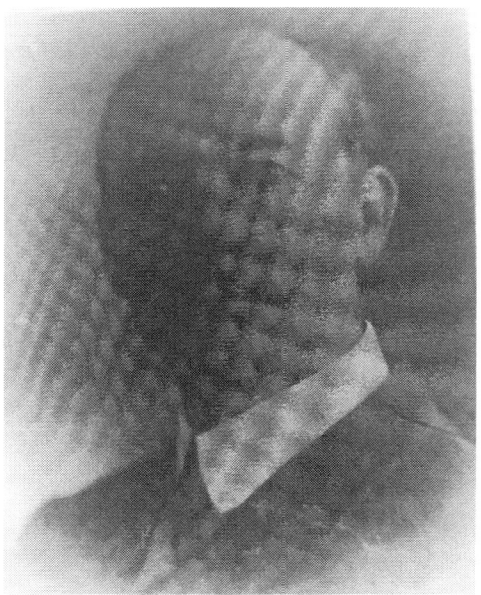

**Rev. P. L. Moseley**
**(New Brockton Baptist's 6th Pastor 1914-1920)**

## The Pastor Associational Years (1920-1924)

The year 1920 witnessed significant renovation both inside and outside the Church, along with property repairs totaling $325.00. October of 1920, Rev. L. A. Nall from Elba, Alabama was called by the Church and served as Pastor for one associational year. The Church's membership grew to an impressive 137. In that same month, Rev. L. A. Nall spoke at the 13th Annual Session of the Coffee County Baptist Association at Clintonville Primitive Baptist Church, Clintonville, Alabama.

October 1921 saw the arrival of Rev. J. A. Seay from Newville, Alabama, who assumed the pastoral duties for one associational year.

In October, 1922, Dr. J. A. Lowery, the President of the Baptist Collegiate Institute in Newton, Alabama, was chosen by the Church and served as Pastor for one associational year. During this time, the Church started purchasing Baptist Young People's Union material. New Brockton Baptist became active in the Women's Missionary Union (W.MU.) and Young People Missionary organizations, with the Young People's being led by Mrs. N. R. Phillips.

In October 1923 the Church chose Rev. R. D. Bevis from Montgomery, Alabama to serve as Pastor for one associational year.

## Rev. Johnson (1924-1928)

In 1924, the Church welcomed Rev. J. S. Johnson, former pastor for FBC Gurley, Gurley, Alabama, answered the call by the Church and served as Pastor. That same year, the venerable Old Church building served the congregation, which had blossomed to encompass over 150 devoted members. Under the visionary leadership of Rev. Johnson, the seed of the Church, sprouted. The location for the new church building was chosen to be at the corner of McKinnon St. and Massy St., now known as Lee St.- The very spot it is located today.[5] The lot was secured from Professor J. J. Langham. The Committee that secured the lot: J. G. Crumpler and J. T. Jones.

The steadfast members of the building committee, comprising H. L. Crabtree, J. A. Wright, and S. D. Fuller worked tirelessly to bring the dream to fruition. Their unwavering dedication and sweat equity culminated in the magnificent completion of the new brick building, an architectural marvel that came to life at a total cost of $13,800.00.

And in the following year 1925, First Baptist Church of New Brockton transitioned into a full-time church for the first time.

**The finish new FBC building in 1925**     **The Church Cornerstone**

On December 12th, 1926, a momentous occasion unfolded as the inaugural dedication of the new church building took place, when the cornerstone was laid, under the leadership of Rev. J. S. Johnson. Just under a year later, on October 21, 1927, Rev. J. S. Johnson spoke at the 20th Annual Session of the Coffee County Baptist Association at New Ebenezer Church, Elba, Alabama.

By 1928 the First Baptist Church of New Brockton witnessed a flourishing congregation that grew its membership to the beautiful number of 313.

---

[5] see Appendix H for Map

## Rev. Bush (1929-1938)

In the following year, 1929, Rev. W. M. Bush from Hartford, Alabama answered the call of the Church to serve as Pastor.

The year 1930 marked a pivotal moment as the Men of the Church banded together to form the Men's Brotherhood, a pioneering achievement not only for the Coffee County Baptist Association but also across the entire state of Alabama. Rev. R. M. Hunter, the esteemed founder of the FBC New Brockton was invited and given special recognition as founder of the Church.

On September 23,1930, The 23rd Annual Session of the Coffee County Baptist Association was held at First Baptist Church of New Brockton. The Speakers were C.S. Thomas, Pastor of FBC Enterprise and FBC News Brockton's very own Pastor Rev. W. M. Bush.

On September 27th,1933, Rev. W. M. Bush delivered a compelling address at the 26th Annual Session of the Coffee County Baptist Association. This significant event took place in the walls of Goodman Baptist Church, in the heart of Goodman, Alabama.

The following year, in 1934, the Pastorium for FBC New Brockton was bought for the sum of $1,200.00, from the owner, S. D. Fuller. This historical site was once the former home of Dr. J. B. Woodall, located on Main Street which is currently known as McKinnon St.

Fast forward to October 1st, 1936, when Rev. W. M. Bush spoke at the 28th Annual Session of the Coffee County Baptist Association at Cool Springs Baptist, Enterprise, Alabama. In 1936 Rev. W. M. Bush baptized a total of 13 souls.

In the summer of 1937, FBC New Brockton embarked on a mission to teach young souls about CHRIST. They organized a Bible School which was held at the New Brockton High School, attracting over 120 children to attend.

**Members of New Brockton Baptist Bible School**

Students who attended the New Brockton Baptist Church Bible Study school are shown in the above photo. Over 120 children were enrolled in the school, which gave instructions in handicraft in addition to a study of the Bible. The Rev. W. M. Bush is pastor of the church.

**FBC New Brockton's Bible School - 1937**
**(Located at New Brockton High School)**

In the fall of 1937, September 29th, Rev. W. M. Bush was called to speak at the 30th Annual Session of the Coffee County Baptist Association at Mt. Olive Baptist Church, Elba, AL. The following year, on November 27th, 1938, Rev. W. M. Bush resigns as Pastor of First Baptist Church of New Brockton, accepting a pastorate at Samson Baptist Church. While he was Pastor for 10 years, New Brockton's Congregation grew from 267 to 450 people.

## Rev. Beasley (1938-1940)

In late 1938, Rev. H. W. Beasley, the pastor of FBC Kinston, Kinston, Alabama, was called by the Church to serve as Pastor. In the fall of 1939, September 27th to 28th, the 31st Annual Session of the Coffee County Baptist Association was held at First Baptist Church of New Brockton. The speakers were Rev. J. D. Willingham spoke on the 27th and Rev. A. W Baker spoke on the 28th.

**Bible in Main Foyer**
**(Current)**

# Chapter 5

# The Church's Golden Age

*"That in the ages to come he might shew the exceeding riches of his grace in his kindness toward us through Christ Jesus."*
**The Epistle to the Ephesians 2:7**

## The Debut of an Age (1940-1941)

In 1940, First Baptist Church of New Brockton initiated Vacation Bible School. Later that December, Rev. E. S. Pate of Bessemer, Alabama, answered the Church's call to become Pastor.

## Rev. Fleming (1941-1944)

In May 1941, Rev. Frank J. Fleming, who had previously served as Pastor at Luverne Baptist Church, Luverne, AL, was summoned by the Church to lead as Pastor at First Baptist Church of New Brockton. On a memorable Friday, June 13th, 1941, Coffee County Missionary Baptist Preachers Society convened, and at 1:30 p.m. Rev. Fleming delivered a powerful sermon from Daniel chapter 11.

In 1942, on October 14th, Rev. F. J. Fleming was invited to speak at the 34th Annual Session of the Coffee County Baptist Association, hosted by Whitewater Baptist Church, Elba, Alabama.

However, a Somber day dawned on March 8th, 1944, as Rev. Frank J. Fleming passed away, leaving First Baptist Church of New Brockton without a Pastor. Until, Rev. J. W. Jones of Deatsville, Alabama, responded to the Church's call to be the Pastor.

## Rev. Jones (1944-1946)

In 1945, on Father's Day, FBC New Brockton organized a special Father's Day Service. Rev. Jones preached a powerful sermon titled "God's Good Man" and the W.M.U.graciously served refreshments afterwards.

On October 18th, 1945, Rev. J. W. Jones made a noteworthy appearance as the speaker at the 37th Annual Session of the Coffee County Baptist Association, hosted by Hebron Baptist Church, Jack, Alabama,

On January 22nd, 1946, The Coffee County Baptist Sunday School Convention took place at First Baptist Church of New Brockton. Then on Sunday, January 27th,1946, Rev. Jones preached a remarkable sermon titled "the Open Door of 1946."

In June, 1946,the First Baptist Church of New Brockton took a cautious approach and postponed the Vacation Bible School due to concern surrounding the Polio Threat.

In July 1946, a memorable Layman's Revival was conducted at the First Baptist Church of New Brockton. E. E. Cox from Birmingham, Alabama, led this inspiring event, leaving a lasting impact on the congregation.

## Rev. Dykes (1947-1952)

February 27th, 1947, Rev. J. Hollan Dykes from Hartford, Alabama, answered the call by the Church to serve as Pastor. Also, this same year, a gas heating system was installed at the price of $1,410.00. Also, the church adopted the unified budget plan for the first time. Regular church bulletins were used for the first time.

**Rev. J. Hollan Dykes**
**(17th Pastor of FBC New Brockton 1947-1952)**

October 16th, 1947, Rev. J. Hollan Dykes was the guest speaker at the 39th Annual Session of the Coffee County Baptist Association at New Hope Baptist, Jack, Alabama, where he gave the Missionary message. Dr. B. R. Justice, FBC Enterprise Pastor, was the Moderator (for the 5th Consecutive year), W.T. Whitman from Elba was the Vice-moderator, J.A. Harris from New Brockton was Clerk. Barbecue was also served afterwards.

In April, 1948, a Revival was conducted at Park Ave. Baptist Church, Enterprise Alabama, by FBC New Brockton's own Rev. Dykes

The next year, in 1949, the Church purchased new pews at the cost of $2,483.05. Later, on the dates of July 10th to 17th that year, a Revival was at

First Baptist of New Brockton, with the guest preacher being Rev. Claude T. Ammerman, Pastor of First Baptist of Troy, Troy, Alabama. The wonderful music led by Rev. Harry W. Hargrove, Pastor of First Baptist of Brundidge, Brundidge, Alabama. On October 13th, 1949, The 41st Annual Session of the Coffee County Baptist Association was held at First Baptist Church of New Brockton. The Speaker was Dr. James Allen Smith, Pastor of County Line Baptist (Dothan Hwy).

On March 29th, 1951, FBC New Brockton joined the Churches of Coffee County in the Evangelistic Crusade.

August 10th, 1952, Revival held at First Baptist of New Brockton, Speaker is Rev. Clarence M. Mezick. Rev. Mezick served as pastor of Bethany Baptist, New Brockton, Alabama and also held the pastoral role at Pastor Damascus Baptist, Elba, Alabama.

In a significant development later that year, in November of 1952, the Church acquired and installed Chimes in its magnificent Church Tower. During his tenure at FBC New Brockton, Rev. J. Hollan Dykes baptized over 33 souls.

**Hymnal Books and Bible**
**(Current)**

# Chapter 6
# The Age of the Great Revivals

*If my people, which are called by my name, shall humble themselves, and pray, and seek my face, and turn from their wicked ways; then will I hear from heaven, and will forgive their sin, and will heal their land.*

The Second Epistle to the Chronicles 7:14

## Rev. Mezick First Tenure

In February of 1953, the Church extended an invitation to Rev. Clarence M. Mezick, who answered the call to serve as Pastor. During this time frame, the Church adopted the budget plan for the *Alabama Baptist*, which was to provide a copy of the *Alabama Baptist* in every home of all the church members.

As a testament to their commitment to the growth of the Church, they purchased new pulpit furniture for the Church. In Rev. Mezick's first 20 months of tenure, he baptized 85 individuals.

On the memorable Friday evening of April 3rd, 1953, the Church convened a special meeting that gathered all the teachers and Officers of the Sunday School at the First Baptist Church of New Brockton. This gathering was for the purpose of devising a strategy to reach the goal of 200 attendance in Sunday School.

Just days later, on the 12th of April that same year, a significant step toward the goal was achieved when 83 people enrolled in Training Union studies.

**Rev. Clarence M. Mezick**

**18th Pastor of FBC New Brockton (1953-1957)**

**&**

**20th Pastor of FBC New Brockton (1958-1964)**

## The Great Spiritual Awakening

In July, 1953, The Great Evangelical movement swept through the Southland. Its impact reverberated through the sacred hall of First Baptist Church of New Brockton. The Divine outpouring of GOD's SPIRIT was nothing but Miraculous, sparking a profound spiritual movement. Rev. Mezick served as the Evangelist for the Revivals, while Rev. L. A. Gable, hailing from Charlotte, North Carolina was the Music Director.

## A Good Problem to Have

As October 4th, 1953, dawned, the rapid growth of the Congregation compelled the Church to acknowledge the pressing need for more room at the Church. The Sunday School surpassed all expectations, swelling from 200 to an astounding 330 attendees, and the Training Union experienced growth, boasting 178 participants. The Sunday School had outgrown the confines of the Church Building, leading the Church to meet in unconventional places such as the City Theater, New Brockton City Hall, and a Warehouse. Recognizing the urgency, the Church unanimously voted and plans were made for an Educational Building to be erected. The Building and Furnishing Committee comprised S. D. Fuller, S. T. Jones, and J. B. Maddox.

On October 20th, 1953, the lot adjacent to the Church building was bought for the Educational Building, securing it from Mrs. J. A. Brock at the cost of $1,504.20.

On January 29th, 1954, the ground was broken for the Educational Building. Unity and dedication from the volunteers dug ditches, hauled sand and unloaded bricks, all free of charge. Materials were bought and delivered to the Church at wholesale price by J. B. Maddox and Colley Pittman Mere. Co.. The grand total for the Building and its furnishings amounted to $31,360.78.

*(Left to Right)*
**(Deacon) John Wallace, Mrs. Wallace and Rev. Mezick**

REV. C. M. MEZICK AND JOHN WALLACE turn the first shovels of dirt in the ground breaking for the educational building for the New Brockton Baptist Church. Others present and shown include W. E. Wilkes, Emmett Sawyer, Leon Bailey, Austin Harris, Jimmy Sawyer, Libby Hayes, James L. Sawyer, Mr. and Mrs. J. K. Hayes, Ray Sawyer, Jonnie Maddox, Bob Herring, Mrs. Geo. Hogg, Mrs. Susie Folsom, Judy Moore, Mr. and Mrs. Nevin Hayes, and Geo. Hogg.

**Groundbreaking on January 20th, 1954**

**Ladies of Missionary Society**

**FBC Deacon and Rev. Mezick**

Holding the shovels of dirt
Rev. Mezick
John Wallace
(The oldest Deacon)

Rev. Mezick praying over the ground breaking

## Calling to the Ministry

On April 28th, 1954, the FBC Youth observed Youth Week and led the services during the week. On May 30th, 1954, Mr. Richard L. Hayes and Mr. James Maddox was given a license to preach by First Baptist Church of New Brockton. Miss Sarah Nell Peacock was selected to do Missionary Work in the Great State of Alabama.

**Richard L. Hayes**

**James Maddox**

**Sarah Nell Peacock**

In June, 1954, First Baptist Church of New Brockton celebrated a significant milestone as they completed the two-story Educational Building. FBC New Brockton's 1954 VBS had 135 enrolled with the average of 126 attending. Shortly thereafter, in July 1954, the congregation welcomed Rev. Richard Hayes as Assistant Pastor for FBC New Brockton. From July 11th to 16th, 1954, a spirited Revival took place at FBC New Brockton, with Rev. Clarence M. Mezick delivered the sermons. During this revival people prayed all night long at the Church, every night. In the last week of July, Miss Martha Will Potts, an African American Missionary to the African American community, spoke at FBC New Brockton, giving her reports in the months of June and July about the African American VBS program in Coffee County, with 620 enrolled, 36 Dedication, and 2 souls coming to CHRIST. She finished up her rally at Poplar Springs Baptist.

On the date of August 15th, 1954, Rev. Richard (Dick) Hayes received his Ordination to the Gospel Ministry from First Baptist Church of New Brockton. The following month, on September 14th, 1954, 7 a.m. Howard College inaugurated the Howard Extension Center at First Baptist Church of New Brockton in the Educational Building. Three courses were offered; New Testament, Preview of the Sunday School Lesson, and English Grammar. The Teachers were Rev. A. O. Martz, the Pastor of Park Ave. Baptist Church, Enterprise, Alabama; Rev. Murray L. Seay, the Pastor of Park Ave. Baptist Church of Elba, Alabama; Rev. J.W. Lester, the Pastor of Mt. Pleasant Baptist Church; Rev. C. M. Mezick, the Pastor of New Brockton Baptist was the Registrar, while Rev. Lester was the Director of the Center.

In September, 1954 Asst. Pastor Rev. Richard Hayes resigned his position to pursue further education in Fort Worth, Texas. On the 23rd of September that same year, the cornerstone of the Educational Building was laid. Then, on September 26rh, 1954, a heartfelt Dedication Service was held for the Educational Building, with Rev. Clarence M. Mezick leading the congregation.

The Dedicatory sermon was eloquently delivered by Rev. James W. Eady, the Pastor of Opp Baptist Church, Opp, Alabama.

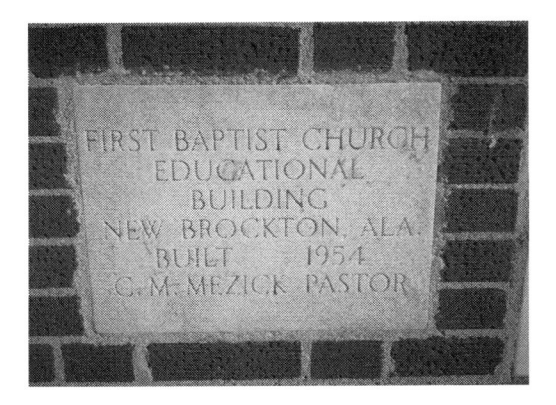

**The Finished Educational Building**   **The Cornerstone of the Educational Building**

On January 11th, 1955, Mr. Eldrid Ellis received his license to preach from FBC New Brockton. On March 6th to 13th, 1955, a Revival was held at First Baptist of New Brockton with a sermon from Dr. James Lee Roy Steel, the Pastor of First Baptist of Opelika, Opelika, Alabama.

In August, 1955, FBC New Brockton suspended its Night Service to lend support to the First Methodist Church of New Brockton's Revival. This spirit of community and cooperation was a testament to FBC New Brockton's commitment to the Gospel being preached to the lost.

On September, 6th, 1955, First Baptist Church of New Brockton opened its doors to Howard College Extension Courses for the second consecutive year in 1955, counting its dedication to education and the faith.

February 12th to 19th, 1956. FBC New Brockrton hosted another impactful revival, featuring Rev. Mezick as speaker. In August of 1956, James C. Mezick, the pastor's son, was ordained to the Gospel ministry by the First Baptist Church of New Brockton, at the request of Oenaville Baptist Church, Waco, Texas.

In November of 1956, the Baptist Brotherhood of Coffee County and the Royal Ambassador had a Banquet at FBC New Brockton, with 160 members attending.

**MEN AND BOYS** — More than 160 members of the Baptist Brotherhood organizations of Coffee County and Royal Ambassadors enjoy chicken at the third annual Brotherhood R. A. Banquet at New Brockton First Baptist Church. Those present represented most of the Baptist Churches of Coffee County. The event was held Friday night. (Eagle Photo)

**Coffee County Baptist Brotherhood Banquet**

As March of 1957 arrived, Dr. James Allen Smith, pastor of County Line Baptist Church near Dothan, Alabama, was called upon by the Church to serve as a Supply Pastor. The decision followed the resignation of Rev. C. M. Mezick, who accepted a call to Mt. Olive Baptist Church, Elba, Alabama. During Rev. Mezick 's first tenure, he baptized over 130 souls.

In June 1957, Dr. John B. Johnson from Warrior, Alabama, answered the call to be the Pastor..

In the years spanning from 1953 to 1957 that marked the Great Spiritual Awakening in First Baptist Church of New Brockton and for the first time in the history of the Church, men and women answered the calling of GOD, for the Ministry and Missionary work.

The individuals that answered the call included Miss Peggy Helms, Miss Sarah Nell Peacock, Miss Linda Lou Jones, Mr. Richard L. Hayes, Mr. James Maddox, Mr. James C. Mezick, Mr. Jimmy D. Sawyer, Mr. Eldrid Ellis and John Ed Sawyer. The Church was privileged to license Mr. Richard L. Hayes, Mr. James Maddox, Mr. James C. Mezick, Mr. Jimmy D. Sawyer, Mr. Eldrid Ellis and John Ed Sawyer to preach. The Church later Ordained three of these young men, Mr. Richard L. Hayes, Mr. James C. Mezick and Mr. Jimmy D. Sawyer.

Additionally, Miss Peggy Helms, Miss Sarah Nell Peacock and Miss Linda Lou Jones advanced their education and pursued Missionary Work. These individuals' devotion and commitment truly enriched the legacy of First Baptist Church of New Brockton during this Miraculous Era in Church History.

**Pulpit**
**(Current)**

James C. Mezick

James Maddox

Linda Lou Jones

Peggy Helms

Sarah Nell Peacock

# Chapter 7
## The Church's Silver Age

*"His glory is great in thy salvation: honour and majesty hast thou laid upon him."*

**The Book of Psalms 21:5**

### Entering the Silver Age

In 1957, the Church acquired the necessary secretarial equipment. Under the leadership of Dr. John B. Johnson, a Church Library, was established and fully equipped, with plans set in motion for its services to the congregation.

**Dr. John B. Johnson**
**19th Pastor of FBC New Brockton**
**(1957-1958)**

In 1958, Chaplain John N. Hudson, the Chaplin of Fort Rucker was called by the Church to serve as the Supply Pastor following the resignation of Dr.. J. B. Johnson. In July of 1958 a Revival was held at FBC New Brockton, with Rev. M.M. Hargrove, Pastor of Siluria Baptist, Alabaster, Alabama, as the Evangelist.

## The Return of Rev. Mezick

In December of 1958, Rev. Clarence M. Mezick returned to once again serve the role of Pastor of First Baptist Church of New Brockton.

The year 1959 witnessed a significant development as air conditioning was installed in the Church. In July of that year, Rev. Richard L. Hayes, pastor of North Side Baptist, Milledgeville, Georgia and former resident of New Brockton was the guest Evangelist of a Revival at FBC New Brockton. Rev. L.A. Gable Jr., Pastor of Derita Baptist, Charlotte, North Carolina, was the song leader.

In February of 1960, Chaplin James D. Sawyer of the U.S. Navy, who had been Ordained by FBC New Brockton, reached out to the Deacons of FBC New Brockton to request the Licensing of Roland C. Money for the Ministry. The Church, by unanimous vote, agreed to receive him as a member of the Church and granted him Licensed to Preach the Gospel under the auspices of FBC New Brockton. That same year, the Church membership swelled to 426, and the Church property was valued at $85,000.00.

On October 13th, 1960, the 52nd Annual Session of the Coffee County Baptist Association convened at First Baptist Church of New Brockton. The Moderator was Rev. John F. Lindsey, the Clerk, was Rev. A. L. Strozier, the speakers included Rev. Q. P. Jones, the Pastor of Bethany Baptist, and Rev. James W. Eady, the Pastor of Mt. Pleasant Baptist

On April 22nd to 28th, 1963, Rev. Mezick was the guest Evangelist for a Revival at Westview Baptist, Enterprise, Alabama. In June of 1963, the VBS had an Average attendance of 93 students. Moving forward to November of 1963, Rev. Mezick typed out a letter to the U.S. Congressmen and Senators from

Alabama, expressing that FBC New Brockton opposed a tax bill. During Rev. Mezick second tenure, he Baptized over 55 souls.

**1963 Vacation Bible School**

**93 Students in attendance**

**Mrs. J.A. Harris - Principal, Rev. Mezick, Mrs. LaRue Broxton, Miss Patricia Hayes, Miss Pat Locklar, and Miss Patricia Lambert**

**First Baptist Church of New Brockton (1960's)**

## Rev. Gales (1964-1966)

In 1964, the Church called Rev. M. T. Gales to serve as its Pastor. On September 24th that same year, the Coffee County Baptist Women's Missionary Society held a prayer retreat at First Baptist Church of New Brockton, with Rev. Gales delivering a sermon from the 17th chapter of the Gospel of John. He encouraged each of the ladies to select Scripture and share personal testimonies, closing the devotion period with the hymn "Teach me to Pray".

The year 1965 saw two more men answering the call to preach: Mr. Silas Shepherd and Mr. W. C. (Bud) Goodson. They received license to preach from the Church, and later, the Church had the privilege of Ordaining them. While Rev. Gales was the Pastor at FBC New Brockton, he baptized over 65 souls.

## Rev. McWhirter (1967-1969)

In 1967, Rev. Frank Carswell McWhirter was called by the Church to serve as the Pastor.

On October 13th, 1969, the 61st Annual Session of the Coffee County Baptist Association was hosted by First Baptist Church of New Brockton, with Rev. Paul Kendrick as the speaker.

## Rev. Raley (1970-1972)

In 1970, Rev. Charles B. Raley answered the call by the Church to serve as the Pastor.

In July, 1971, a revival was held at FBC New Brockton, with Rev. Lester Garrett, Pastor of First Baptist Church of Level Plains, Level Plains, Alabama, was the speaker, and FBC New Brockton's own Wendall Rodgers led the music.

On October 15th, 1971, Rev. Charles B. Raley addressed the 63rd Annual Session of the Coffee County Baptist Association at Calvary Baptist Church, Enterprise, Alabama.

In March, 1972, an inspiring revival was held at FBC New Brockton during Homecoming Sunday. Rev. J.D. Kelly, the esteemed pastor of Southside Baptist, Montgomery, Alabama, as the Evangelist. The Music was expertly led by Ronnie Driver.

In April, 1972, FBC New Brockton ventured to compete in a Volleyball Tournament in the Non-Student Division, against such opponents as St. Luke Methodist, in Enterprise, Alabama; West Gate AG, in Enterprise, Alabama; Meddacs, in Fort Rucker, Alabama; Smoke & Rockets, in Fort Rucker, Alabama; Dothan Air Guard; ESJC Faculty; Prattville YMCA, in Prattville, Alabama; and Enterprise Lions Club.

October 13th, 1972, The 64th Annual Session of the Coffee County Baptist Association convened at First Baptist Church of New Brockton, featuring Rev. Alfred Ikner, the pastor of Goodman Baptist as the speaker. During Rev. Raley's tenure at FBC New Brockton, he baptized over 64 souls.

## Rev. Croft (1973-1974)

In 1973, Rev. Colbert Croft answered the Church's call to serve as the Pastor.

**Rev Colbert & Mrs. Joyce Croft**
**24th Pastor of FBC New Brockton (1973-1974)**

## End of an Age

In 1975, Rev. Howard Jones answered the call from the Church to serve as the Interim Pastor for a short period. Also, during the same year, Rev. David Richburg, the former Pastor of FBC Robertsdale, Baldwin County, answered the Church's call to serve as the Pastor.

**Rev. David & Mary Richburg, Marica and David II**

**FBC New Brockton Deacons (1978)**
(Front Row, Left to Right)
**Jimmy Peacock, Austin Harris & Ralph Bruce**
(Back Row, Left to Right)
**Leon Roberts, J.K. Hayes, Rufus McKinney & George Hogg**
Not Shown
**Wendall Rodgers & Claude Sawyer**

Rev. Richburg fulfilled the role of the Moderator for the Coffee County Baptist Association from 1971 to 1973 before coming to FBC New Brockton. Notably, in July of 1978, FBC New Brockton held a revival service, with Rev. Eugene Lloyd, Pastor of David St. Baptist, Greenville, South Carolina being the Evangelist.

**Rev. David Richurg**

**25th Pastor of FBC New Brockton (1976-1979)**

# Chapter 8
## The Renovation Period

*And they that shall be of thee shall build the old waste places: thou shalt raise up the foundations of many generations; and thou shalt be called, The repairer of the breach, The restorer of paths to dwell in.*
**The Book of Isaiah 58:14**

### Rev. Henderson

In 1980, Rev. Rex Edmon Henderson from Houston County, Alabama, was called to be the Pastor by the Church. With the aim of safeguarding the leadership of the Church from potential legal liabilities in a changing world, and to enhance its overall operational readiness, the Church was incorporated as First Baptist Church of New Brockton, Inc.

**Rev. Rex E. Henderson**
**26th Pastor of FBC New Brockton**

On October 21st, 1983, Rev. Rex Henderson delivered a powerful sermon during the 75th Annual Session of the Coffee County Baptist Association, hosted at the esteemed Kinston Baptist Church, Kinston, Alabama.

Between 1980 to 1987 the congregation saw a remarkable growth in its membership to 528. The congregation voted to completely renovate all the church facilities. It was done in three phases with the total cost at $185,000. When all three phases were completed, the Church's appraised value was $585,000.

## Renovation

On September 20th, 1987, at 11 a.m. a Special Dedication Service was held for the newly renovated facilities. Dr. Don Watterson, Associate Executive Secretary of the Alabama Baptist State Convention, delivered the message.

**FBC New Brockton before Renovation**

**FBC New Brockton after Renovation**

In 1989, the Church extended its call to Rev. Mack King, to serve as Interim Pastor for a brief period. Later that same year, the Church welcomed Rev. David Atchison as Pastor. During this time, the Pastor's Sunday School Class and the Children's Worship were both established.

**FBC New Brockton Sanctuary after the Renovation**

## Rev. Barr (1993-1999)

In 1993, Rev. Ken May answered the call of the Church to serve as Interim Pastor for a short time. Later that year, the Church called upon Rev. Robert "Bob" Barr from Pike County, Alabama, to serve as the Pastor.

**Rev. Robert "Bob" Barr**

In 1994, the Church made an acquisition, purchasing a van. From October 30th to November 2nd, 1995, a significant revival took place at FBC New Brockton, which was preached by Rev. Garry Winstead, Pastor of Ino Baptist Church.

In 1996, the esteemed Dr. John Granger, Pastor of Goodman Baptist, Goodman, Alabama, conducted the Winter Bible Study sessions at First Baptist Church of New Brockton. On May 6th, 1996, the Southeast Alabama Minister Conference convened at FBC New Brockton, featuring Dr. Ted Traylor, the pastor of Mt. Olive Baptist, Pensacola, Florida as the key speaker.

In 1997, a noteworthy ministry was launched, the Van Ministry, which played an important role in transportation of children in the community to Sunday School and Church.

In the fall of 1999, Rev. Carlton Moore was called by the Church and served as Interim Pastor.

**FBC New Brockton (2000)**

# Chapter 9

# The Centennial year

*In hope of eternal life, which God, who never lies, promised before the ages began.*

**The Epistle to Titus 1:2**

## Y2K

In the year 2000, often referred to as Y2K, a sense of new beginnings swept through the Community, including the Church. It was during this time that Dr. Jim H. Strength was called to serve as the new Pastor in the month of June.

In September, 2001, the Church called Rev. Henry Johnson to serve as Interim Pastor.

## Centennial Celebration

Then, on the date August 25th, 2002, First Baptist Church of New Brcockton Celebrated the "100 year - Centennial Celebration." The service started at 10 a.m. that Sunday morning, with Jon Blissitte leading the Service in the Morning Prayer. With warm words of welcoming message extended from Wendell Rodgers, with the musical talents of Anthony Stewart, Rev. & Mrs. Crolbert Croft the Church was uplifted. Billy Tindol gave recognition to former Pastors, Dr. John Granger from the Coffee County Baptist Association read the Scripture, Dr. Joe Talmadge from the Alabama Historical Commission, Rev. John Sawyer from the Alabama Baptist Convention both gave a speech and Rev. Henry Johnson preached.

## Rev. Hixson

In 2003, the Church extended a call for Rev. Chad Hixson to serve the role of Head Pastor, and he embraced the calling.

Rev. Chad Hixson

**30th Pastor of FBC New Brockton (2003-2008)**

## Rev. Stinson

In November of 2008, Rev. Slade Stinson answered the call by the Church to serve as Pastor.

**Rev. Slade Stinson**

**31st Pastor of FBC New Brockton (2008-2010)**

On September 12th, 2009, FBC New Brockton hosted an outdoor extravaganza in collaboration with M.U.D. Ministries, drawing sports enthusiasts and families of all generations. Revival started the next day on September 13th to 16th with Evangelist Eric Hixson of M.U.D. Ministries guest speaking.

The following year, in 2010, Dr. Ernest Bailey answered the call to serve as Interim Pastor for FBC New Brockton.

**FBC New Brockton (2022)**

**FBC New Brockton (2022)**

# Chapter 10
## Dusk

*"Shew us thy mercy, O Lord, and grant us thy salvation."*

The Book of Psalms 85:4

## Rev. Sims

In November of 2011, the Church called upon Rev. Nathan Sims to serve as Pastor.

**Rev. Nathan Sims**
**32nd Pastor of FBC New Brockton (2011-2022)**

From March 11th to 14th, 2012, an inspiring Revival Service took place at FBC New Brockton, featuring Rev. Chad Hixson as the speaker & Craig Stringfield as the worship leader.

In October 2012, Hal Yarbrough began serving as the Minister of Music at FBC New Brockton.

In 2013, Edith King began serving as Pianist for the Church. From March 10th to 13th, 2013, a Revival Service was conducted by Rev. Ronnie Smith as the Evangelist, accompanied by the Worship Leaders Hal Yarbrough, Lloyd Helms and Tim Willis. During the same year, the windows in the Sanctuary and across the back of the Church Building were replaced.

**Wiley & Edith King**

From March 16th to 19th, 2014, a Revival Service took place at FBC New Brockton, with Rev. Stacy Stafford, the Pastor of Southside Baptist Church, Dothan, Alabama, as the speaker, and Kevin Cobb, the Worship Pastor of Southside Baptist Church, Dothan, Alabama, leading the worship.

From April 10th to 13th, 2016, another Revival Service graced FBC New Brockton, with Rev. "Buddy" Hood, the Pastor of Hartford Baptist Church,

Hartford, Alabama, as the Evangelist and FBC New Brockton's own Minister of Music Hal Yarbrough leading worship.

## The Joint Revivals

Then, from March 19th to 22nd, 2017, a Joint Revival Service was held with Calvary Baptist Church, Enterprise, Alabama, with Rev. Shawn Bentley, pastor of FBC Gantt, Gantt, Alabama, as the Evangelist, while Dr. Roger Walworth of FBC Fort Payne, Fort Payne, Alabama presided over the worship. During the Fall of that year, in October, Wiley King began to serve as Stand-In Music Minister. In November 2017, the Pastor Rev. Sims moved out of the Pastorium, which was 112 N. Lee St., and bought his own home in Enterprise, Alabama.

In February 2018, from the 25th to 28th, another Joint Revival Service was held again with Calvary Baptist Church, Enterprise, Alabama, with international Evangelist Don Graham from Clanton, Alabama, being the speaker, while Chris Diffey, the Music Minister from Lakeside Baptist, Birmingham, Alabama, was the Worship Leader. In April of 2018, the Church voted as a collective to sell the Pastorium.

A Joint Revival Services was once again held with Calvary Baptist Church, Enterprise, Alabama, from February 17th to 20th, 2019, with Dr. Tim Cox was the guest speaker, while Rev. Craig Stringfield was the Worship Leader. In May of 2019, the Pastorium was sold. That Summer, the Vacation Bible School (VBS) was transformed into a Summer Youth Retreat due to the reduced number of children attending Church.

## COVID

In early 2020, the world was gripped by fear surrounding a new pandemic, COVID-19. From February 9th to 12th of that year, a Joint Revival Service once again united Calvary Baptist Church, Enterprise, Alabama, with Evangelist Don Graham, from Clanton, Alabama, leading the Revival, while Rev. Danny Williams, the Minister of Music from Mt. Gilead Baptist, Dothan Alabama, serving as the Worship Leader.

As the situation escalated, on March 28th, 2020, Gov. Kay Ivey announced the closure of businesses in response to the COVID-19 crisis. By April 4rh, Gov. Ivey issued a Stay at Home Order, closing schools, beaches and nonessential business, all in an effort to combat the virus. Due to this, churches all over the Great State of Alabama closed.

The Summer of 2020 brought further disruption as the Summer Youth Retreat was canceled due to the ongoing pandemic.

In May, 2022, Rev. Sims, resigned as Head Pastor of First Baptist of New Brockton, leaving Deacon Doug Nolin, Mrs. Sharon Walker and Mrs. Janice Holloway as the Pastoral Search Committee.

## The Twilight before the Dawn

In June of 2022 Rev. Leon Adams, the former Pastor of Park Ave. Baptist Church of Enterprise, Alabama, along with Dr. John Granger, the esteemed Pastor of The Church on Boll Weevil Circle in Enterprise, delivered sermons for FBC New Brockton's congregation every Sunday morning in the absence of a Pastor. Kay Clark from New Home Baptist Church took the role of Sound Director for a temporary time. While Jan Moore from Damascus Baptist Church graced the Church with her musical talents as a pianist during this time.

On the Memorable day of July 17th, 2022, Bro. Stephen Pope, the Youth Pastor of Damascus Baptist Church, delivered a powerful sermon on John 3:16 that left a lasting impact. As we moved into August of 2022, the Church made a decision to entrust Kyle A. Strickland with the responsibility of establishing the online presence through the creation of the Church's Website and Social Media Accounts.

The turning point came on September 25th when the Church overwhelmingly voted to welcome Rev. Stephen Pope to be the new Pastor. In October, Chuck Nelson stepped forward to lead music during Sunday Morning Worship. To top off the month, the Church participated in "Light the Night," a delightful fall festival in the Town of New Brockton. This wonderful event was spearheaded by Rev. Anthony Sherrer, the Head Pastor of Connect Church, who received support from other congregations, including Coffee County Cowboy Church, Damascus Baptist and Bethany Baptist.

**FBC New Brockton (2022)**

## Chapter 11
# A Dawn of a New Era

### Rev. Pope

On November 6th, 2022, Rev. Stephen Pope commenced his leadership as Head Pastor of FBC New Brockton with a powerful sermon that began with his personal testimony and concluded with a message from Luke 15:11-24. Rev. Pope initiated monthly Growth Meetings to gather ideas aimed at expanding the Church's reach into the community.

### Christmas Time

On December 3rd, FBC New Brockton took part in the New Brockton Christmas Parade by adorning a float that they made.

**Rev. Pope on the Christmas Float**

**The Christmas Float in the Parade**

On December 4th, Harmony Baptist Church graced FBC New Brockton with a beautiful Christmas Cantata.

**Harmony Baptist Church's Christmas Cantata**

On December the 7th, FBC New Brockton reinstated Wednesday Night Service, with Mrs. Jennifer Pope as the Youth Leader overseeing One Way Youth Ministries.

On December 14th, Damascus Baptist Church performed an enchanting Christmas Cantata at FBC New Brockton, and on December 24th, a heartwarming Christmas Eve candlelight Service was held.

**Damascus Baptist Church's Christmas Cantata**

**2023 Christmas Eve Candlelight Service**

**2023 Christmas Eve Candlelight Service**

## A New Year

In January of 2023, the Church reinstated the Choir under the leadership of Chuck Nelson, as Choir Director.

On February 11th, FBC New Brockton hosted in the Fellowship Hall a delightful Valentine's Day Banquet prepared by Mrs. Vicky Harrison. Additionally, on February 26th, the Men's Ministry was inaugurated.

March 26th marked Harmony Baptist Church's captivating Easter Cantata performance. On April 6th, the Church conducted the Lord's Supper Service.

In May of 2023, the men of the Church, including Chuck Hogan, Kyle Strickland, Rod "Wolf" Steiner, Chuck Nelson, Dale Nolin, Noah Nolin, Phil Freese and Johnny Donaldson, began a tradition of praying for the Rev. Stephen Pope before every Sunday Morning Church Service.

## Summer 2023

From June 5th to 10th, the One Way Student Ministries attended the MFuge retreat, where Rev. Stephen and Mrs. Jennifer Pope accompanied them.

**Bro. Stephen & Mrs Jennifer Pope**          **2023 MFuge**

**2023 MFuge**
**FBC New Brockton Youth Group**
**"One Way"**

Later, from June 25th to 28th, FBC New Brockton joyously hosted Vacation Bible School (VBS) for the first time in five years, with Mrs. Danielle Donaldson serving as the VBS Superintendent.

**Bro. Stephen with Pie in his face**      **Statuary decorated for VBS**

**2023 Vacation Bible School**

During the summer of 2023, the women of the Church restored the W.M.U. at FBC New Brockton, with Midge Hogan as the W.M.U. President. The Church also voted to honor Doug Nolin and Jon Blissitte as Deacon Emeritus.

**Church Service**

In September 2023, the Men's Ministry embarked on a project to establish a Blessing Box. The inspiration came from the example set by Calvary Baptist Church in Brenham, Texas, under the leadership of Rev. Billy Sutherland. At

Calvary Baptist, the youth, led by Christina Werlein, where they passionately serve their community with the Blessing Box.

In the brief span of Rev. Pope's Tenure, he has had the privilege of baptizing six souls, while there has been a 358% increase in Church attendance, with 43 people on average attending the Sunday Morning Worship Service.

**Rev. Stephen Pope & Mrs. Jennifer Pope**
**33rd Pastor of FBC New Brockton**

# Chapter 12
## The Pastor's Vision

During my conversation, Bro. Stephen Pope, I had the privilege of inquiring what his vision for FBC New Brockton was. He eloquently responded, "My vision is what God's vision is".

Bro. Stephen, a youthful 38 year-old who is embarking on his first year as a pastor, openly shared his aspirations. His vision is to transform the Church into a beacon of love and to a light to the town of New Brockton with Christ's radiance.

His deep desire is to dispel the prevailing misconceptions about today's American Churches and challenge the stereotype that our focus is solely on outward appearances. Instead, he envisions a Church where people are eager to serve and worship with passion. "I want to see people get involved and on the fire, and then we will see the Church grow."

Brother Stephen also humbly acknowledged the wisdom he had gained from his mentors, including Dr. John Granger, the pastor of Mt. Zion Baptist; Rev. Steve Watson, the pastor of Damascus Baptist; and Rev. Scott Donaldson, his father and the pastor of Harmony Baptist Church. Rev. Scott taught him this profound statement: "Preach the Word and Love the People."

He expressed that while things might change for the better at FBC New Brockton in the future, one unwavering truth remains - the unwavering commitment to preach the True Gospel. This encompasses the belief that

CHRIST is the sole path to heaven, that CHRIST sacrificed HIMSELF for our sins, and that HE triumphantly rose on the third day.

Regarding community engagement, he passionately shared, "As a Former Youth Pastor, my heart resonates with the students, and I aspire to establish a presence at New Brockton Elementary, New Brockton Middle, and New Brockton High School. It is essential that we extend our influence into all these educational institutions." He articulated his desire to engage with teachers from each school on a weekly basis, offering support through ministry and prayer.

He further elaborated on the Church's ongoing efforts to extend its outreach to the community. Initiatives such as the Blessing Box, actively managed by the Men's Ministry, and collaboration with Hand UP for the food pantry are currently underway.

His vision extends to an annual week-long Student Outreach program right here in New Brockton, where youth can serve and minister to the local community. He also envisions an expansion of both Women's (W.M.U.) and Men's Ministries to enable more notable community service.

Concluding, he emphasized, "Being GOD's people, it does not start and stop at 11 o'clock and 12 o'clock on Sunday mornings."

Throughout the interview, his unwavering passion for not just FBC New Brockton, but the Church as a whole, as the Bride of his LORD and Savior JESUS CHRIST, was palpable. This closing quote encapsulates his mission, "We need to develop our hearts for GOD, and to make sure people see it…. We want to share what we have in CHRIST with other people so they can have it, too."

## Chapter 13
# The Author's Commentary

Since my very first day at FBC New Brockton on June 12th, 2022, I've experienced an incredibly warm and inviting atmosphere. At that time, the church had a relatively small congregation, and Rev. Nate had recently stepped down as the pastor. Sunday mornings consisted of Senior Ladies Sunday School and Morning Worship Service, and at the end of every month, we enjoyed Family Night on Wednesday evenings.

During my initial visit, there was no Pastor or Song Leader present, but the Coffee County Baptist Association had sent Dr. Granger to deliver a sermon, and Mrs. Kay Clark led us in song. In the subsequent Sundays, Rev. Leon Adams took the pulpit after Dr. Grainger.

Rumors circulated around town about the church possibly closing its doors, but there was an unmistakable sense in the air – a determination not to give up. It wasn't just about not giving up on the church; it was about the church's commitment to its community.

I developed a deep fascination for delving into the church's history, a journey that led me to unearth hidden aspects and traces of its past. The more I explored, the clearer it became how this church played a pivotal role in God's plan to connect with the community.

During my research, I witnessed a remarkable spark within the church, and the turning point was the calling of Brother Steven Pope as the Head Pastor. His leadership breathed new life into the congregation, igniting an enthusiasm among the Church members.

This renewed energy was undeniably the result of the S‍pirit moving, with people humbly praying on their knees for the church's well-being. I observed the men of the church uniting every Sunday morning to pray fervently for the pastor before the morning service.

Allow me to provide some insight into how our tradition of praying for our pastor before the morning service began. It all started with a close friend of mine, Reverend Joshua Whitaker, who serves as the pastor of the Calvary Baptist Church of Butler, Alabama. He suggested the idea of gathering together in prayer for our pastor. Intrigued by this suggestion, I approached Chuck Hogan and shared Reverend Whitaker's idea with him. To my amazement, Chuck Hogan expressed that the Holy Spirit had been prompting him to initiate the same practice.

Speaking of Chuck Hogan, he is truly a remarkable individual, a force to be reckoned with. His life exudes a divine calling, and his unwavering passion for ministry is undeniable.

We are blessed to have dedicated individuals like Chuck Nelson, whose devotion to music uplifts and praises God. There's also Mrs. Jennifer Pope, whose passion and leadership are instrumental in guiding our youth. Sharon Walker brings a wealth of knowledge and an innate desire to teach, while Mrs. Anne Reynolds exhibits remarkable skill on the piano. Additionally, Mrs. Vicky Harrison's culinary talents in the kitchen are a true gift, and let's not forget about Brother Steven Pope, whose burning desire is to spread the Word of God, the Gospel message, and the love of Christ to a lost world.

Each of these individuals and many others possesses a unique ministry and calling, yet together, they do not merely exist as separate entities. Instead, they stand united as the First Baptist Church of New Brockton—a shining beacon not only for our town but for the entire world.

## Chapter 14
# FBC New Brockton

### Deacons

The Deaconry of FBC New Brockton has been an integral part of the Church since its inception, spanning generations from our very first Deacon, Bro. E.G. Brunson, to S.D Fuller, Lee Brown, Claude Sawyer, Stanley Walker, Jon Blissittee, to name a few and to our dedicated Deacon Bro. Doug Nolin today. Over the course of 120+ years, we've been blessed with the service of more than 77 Deacons who have tirelessly served our community, pastors, and congregation. The Deacons of FBC New Brockton stands as an enduring pillar of strength in the heart of the New Brockton Community.

The role of Deacons holds profound significance within the Christian Faith, playing an indispensable role in the life of the Christian Church. Scripture, as exemplified in Acts of the Apostles 6:1-6, underscores the vital necessity of Deacons. Their primary mission is to assist the pastor with tending to the diverse needs of the Congregation.

### Men's Brotherhood

The Brotherhood at FBC New Brockton stands as an enduring pillar within the vibrant fabric of both the New Brockton community and Coffee County. The pioneering spirit that dates back to the late 1920s and early 1930s, FBC New Brockton was the vanguard among churches in Coffee County, establishing the first Brotherhood of Men. Their influence rippled throughout the state of

Alabama, inspiring numerous other churches to establish Brotherhood Ministries of their own.

In fact, it is believed that FBC New Brockton was not only among the first but perhaps the very first church in Alabama to inaugurate such a Brotherhood. During a time when many churches were unable to create a Brotherhood, FBC New Brockton, along with Bethany Baptist, stood as a rare exception. Presently, FBC New Brockton no longer maintains a Men's Brotherhood Ministry.

## FBC Choir

FBC New Brockton has a rich history of worshiping GOD through the power of music. From its peak in 1956, boasting a choir of 50 members, to the unwavering musical dedication of Wendall Rodgers, Ralph Herring, S.T. Jone and Jerry Griffin, to name a few, the FBC Choir continues to thrive under the passionate leadership of Chuck Nelson.

## The W.M.U.

The Women's Missionary Union (W.M.U.) stands as one of the most prominent mission organizations within the Protestant faith. Its origins trace back to the late 1800s when it was established by the Southern Baptist Convention. In 1905, within the heart of our community, FBC New Brockton birthed the Ladies Aid group under the guidance of Mrs. Rosa Hunter. As time progressed, the Ladies Aid evolved into the formidable W.M.U. By the 1920s, their profound influence began to resonate.

For well over a century, these dedicated women have been instrumental in shaping and upholding the New Brockton community. Esteemed leaders such as Pauline Fuller, Trixie Harris, Reba Blissitte, Sharon Walker, Patt Driggers, and

Betty Miller, among others, have left an indelible mark. Today, Midge Hogan leads the W.M.U. at FBC New Brockton as its President, carrying on the tradition of service and devotion.

## Sunday School

At FBC New Brockton, Sunday School stands as the cornerstone of the efforts towards equipping and discipling the congregation. Sunday School classes are thoughtfully arranged to foster an inclusive and welcoming atmosphere, allowing for every individual to feel connected. Embarking on a journey of spiritual growth, delving into the timeless teachings of the Word of God. The classes cater to individuals of all ages, and we are eager to assist you in finding the perfect class and community to call home.

## Vacation Bible School

In 1964, FBC New Brockton's VBS successfully enlightened and inspired a multitude of individuals about the transformative and redemptive power of Jesus Christ, boasting an impressive enrollment of 156 and an average attendance of 135, setting a remarkable record. With esteemed VBS Superintendence from Rev. Dykes, Dr. Johnson, Miss Linda Jones, Janice Holloway, and Danielle Donaldson to name a few.

## Youth Group

From its beginning in October of 1922, FBC New Brockton's youth has been a force to be reckoned with. From the Youth weeks to the young people stepping into ministries. They have been passionate about becoming devoted followers of CHRIST. With the most recent Student Ministries led by Mrs. Jennfier Pope, called One Way Student Ministries.

FBC New Brockton's approach is centered around biblical teaching and practical applications that are relevant to the daily lives of the students. By offering creative series topics, they aim to keep the students engaged and excited about their spiritual growth. They believe that equipping the teens with the truth will empower them to live out their faith and share it with others, which is why they offer opportunities for them to serve and share the Gospel with their peers. All of this is rooted in our foundational verse from John 14:6, which declares that JESUS is the Way, the Truth, and the Life, and that no one can come to the FATHER except through HIM.

## Men's Ministry

While currently lacking a dedicated Baptist Men's Brotherhood, FBC New Brockton proudly boasts a vibrant Men's Ministry under the capable leadership of Reverend Stephen Pope and Chuck Nelson. This dynamic group comprises numerous dedicated individuals, including Chuck Hogan, Kyle Strickland, Rod "Wolf" Steiner, Dale Nolin, Noah Nolin, Phil Freese, and Ben Pope, all enthusiastically initiating community outreach projects such as the creation of a Blessing Box for the New Brockton community.

# Chapter 15
## The Gospel

If you have not heard what the Gospel is yet, The word Gospel is Old English for Good News. Before I tell you the Good News, I have to tell you the Bad News. The Bad News is that we are sinful people, have all sinned and fell short of the Glory of GOD, we are wretched, none of are good, no not one, and our righteousness is like a filthy rag before a Justice, Holy, and Righteous GOD.

There is no good work or good deeds we can do to earn the right standing before GOD. The wage of Sin is death that means someone has to die for that sin, and that is Hell itself.

**BUT**

This is the good news aka the Gospel. CHRIST came as a perfect MAN, perfect GOD, born of a Virgin, lived a perfect sinless life and went to Calvary and dying for our sins, laying HIS life down to take or condemnation so we can take HIS Righteousness, was buried in a borrowed tomb and rose from the dead on the Third day conquering death and the grave.

If you confess with your mouth that JESUS CHRIST is the LORD and believe in your heart that GOD raised HIM from the dead, you will be saved. We are not promised tomorrow. You can step into an eternity at any second. HE stands at the door of your heart and knocks. The question is, are you going to answer?

Nothing else can save you. Mohammed can't save you, Buddha or the Virgin Mary can not save you, the Pope or your Pastor cannot save you, only the shed Blood of CHRIST can save you.

If you have already answered the calling to Salvation, go share the Gospel, it is the marching orders from our LORD, and also get yourself involved in a local Church body so you can be disciplined and so you can serve others.

# Recommended Reading

Alabama Historical Commission • *"Alabama's Tapestry of Historic Places"* • (1978)

Allen, Lee N., • *"Notable Past Bright Future 1893-1993 First Baptist Church Enterprise, Alabama* • (1993

Day, Amelia Herring • *"A Quilt of Memories from a place called Home. New Brockton, Alabama"* • (2010)

Flynt, Wayne • *"Alabama Baptist, Southern Baptist in the Heart of Dixie"* • (1998)

Heritage Publishing Consultant, Inc. • *"The Heritage of Coffee County, Alabama"* • (2002)

History Committee • *"History of Coffee County Baptists Association, New Brockton, Alabama 1998-2002"* • (2002)

Keach, Benjamin • *"Keach's Catechism"* • (1851)

New South Associates • *"Boll Weevils, Peanuts, and Air Power: An Architectural and Historical Survey of the City of Enterprise"* • (2002)

Shoffner, Roy, • *"Go Ye Therefore…" History of the Coffee County Baptist Association 1981-1998"* • (1998)

Strozier, Albert L., • *"Coffee County Baptists, History of the Coffee County Baptist Association of Alabama and of the forty-five members of the Body"* • (1981)

*"The Bible"*

*"The Baptist Confession of Faith & the Baptist Catechism"*

Watson, Fred S., • *"Coffee Grounds, A History of the Coffee County, Alabama 1941-1970"* • (1970)

Whitley, W.T. • *"The Works of John Smyth; Volume 1"* • (1915)

Whitley, W.T. • *"The Works of John Smyth; Volume 2"* • (1915)

Wilson, Mabel Ponder; Woofyerd, Dorothy Youngblood; Busby, Rosa Lee • *"Some Early Alabama Churches,"* • (1973)

# Appendix A
## Pastors

1. Rev. Critten Livingston Matthews - July 1902 - June 1905 (3 years)
2. Rev. Robert Macon Hunter - Summer of 1905 - December, 1907 (2 ½ years)
3. Rev. Critten Livingston Matthews - December, 1907 - Summer 1908 (½ year)
  - **Vacant** - **Summer of 1908 - November 1908** **(½ year)**
4. Rev. Dallas P. Lee - November 1908 - November 1909 (1 year)
5. Rev. J. M. Loftin - November 1909 - 1914 (5 years)
6. Rev. Pope Lloyd Moseley - 1914 - October 1920 (6 years)
7. Rev. L. A. Nall - October 1920 - October 1921 (one associational year)
8. Rev. J. A. Seay - October 1921 - October 1922 (one associational year)
9. Dr.. J. A. Lowery - October 1922 - October 1923 (one associational year)
10. Rev. R. D. Bevis - October 1923 - October 1924 (one associational year)
11. Rev. J. S. Johnson - October 1924 - 1928 (4 years)
12. Rev. W. M. Bush - 1928 - November 1938 (10 years)
13. Rev. H. W. Beasley - 1938 - 1940 (2 years)
14. Rev. E. S. Pate - December 1940 - May 1941 (½ year)
15. Rev. Frank J. Fleming - May 1941 - March 1944 (3 years)
16. Rev. J. W. Jones - 1944 - 1946 (2 years)
17. Rev. J. H. Dykes - 1947 - 1952 (5 years)
18. Rev. Clarence M. Mezick - 1953 - March 1957 (4 years)
  - Dr. James Allen Smith - March 1957 - June 1957 **(Supply Pastor)** (¼ year)
19. Rev. John. B. Johnson - 1957 - 1958 (1 year)
  - Chaplin John N. Hudson - 1958 - December 1958 **(Supply Pastor)** (Less than a Year)
20. Rev. Clarence M. Mezick - December 1958 - 1964 (6 years)
21. Rev. M. T. Gales - 1964 - 1966 (2 years)
22. Rev. Frank McWhirter - 1967 - 1969 (2 years)
23. Rev. Charles Raley - 1970 - 1972 (2 years)
24. Rev. Colbert Croft - 1973 - 1974 (1 year)
  - Rev. Howard Jones - 1975 **(Interim)** (1 year)
25. Rev. David Richburg - 1976 - 1979 (3 years)
  - **Vacant** - **1979 - 1980** **(1 year ?)**
26. Rev. Rex Henderson - 1980 - 1988 (8 years)
  - Rev. Mack King - 1989 **(Interim)** (Less than a year)
27. Rev. David Atchison - 1989 - 1993 (3 years)
  - Rev. Ken May - 1993 **(Interim)** (Less than a year)
28. Rev. Bob Barr - 1993 - July 1999 (6 years)
  - Rev. Carlton Moore - October 1999 - May 2000 **(Interim)** (1 year)
29. Dr. Jim H. Strength - June 2000 - August 2001 (1 year)
  - Rev. Henry Johnson - September 2001 - July 2003 **(Interim)** (2 years)
30. Rev. Chad Hixson - July 2003 - August 2008 (5 years)
31. Rev. Slade Stinson - November 2008 - 2010 (2 years)
  - Dr. Ernest Bailey - 2010 - October 2011 **(Interim)** (1 year)
32. Rev. Nathan Sims - November 2011 - May 2022 (11 years)
  - Rev. Leon Adams - June 2022 - October 2022 **(Interim)** (5 months)
33. Rev. Stephen Pope - November 2022 - Present (Current)

## Appendix B
**Charter Members**

# **Founding Members**

Mr. and Mrs. W. B. Harper

Mr. and Mrs. E. G. Brunson

Mr. and Mrs. Dock Taylor

Rev. and Mrs. J. M. Moore

Miss Bertie Brunson

Miss Bessie Brunson

Miss Berchie McGee

Mrs. Malissa Marsh

Mr. Ed Brunson

# Appendix C
## FBC New Brockton's Deacons

| | | |
|---|---|---|
| L. A. Adkison | B.E. Harris | Leon Roberts |
| J.Leon Bailey | J.A. Harris | Wendell Rodgers |
| Jon Blissitte | Hut Hayes | Wink Rodgers |
| Bill Boland | J.K. Hayes | Claude Sawyer |
| C.C. Brabham | Ralph H. Herring | E.A. Sawyer |
| E. D. Brooks | William Hilyer | Glen Sawyer |
| Lee Brown | George H. Hogg | James L. Sawyer |
| Ralph Bruce | J.L. Hogan | R. Scheffer |
| Steve Bruce | Dwight Holley | B. Silas Shepard |
| E.G. Brunson | Lance Holloway | Huey Sipper |
| Dr. D.A. Bush | J.F. Jones | Douglas Smith |
| Joe E. Clark | L.F. Jones | Jim Bob Striplin |
| Ed Cordie | Seth T. Jones | Jim Stokes |
| F. A. Davis | W.C. Jones | Bill Tindol, Sr. |
| Wesley DeVane | Charlie N. Lockard | Bill Tindol |
| William Bruce DeVaughn | Rusty Lockard | Kenneth Walden |
| W. Hugo DeVaughn | Gibbs McCormick | Stanley Walker |
| Johnny Donaldson | Chuck McGlotherin | John N. Wallace |
| Harold Foster | Rufus McKinney | Phillip Weaver |
| J.D. Fuller | Frank Martin | Lester Whaley |
| S.D. Fuller | R. S. Martin | W.E. Wilkes |
| Leslie Griffin | Steve Musser | Brantley Williams |
| W.C. Goodson | Doug Nolin | Mike Windam |
| Guy F. Gunter Sr. | Jimmy Peacock | J.B. Woodall |
| Andy Harris | Colley E. Pittman | J.A. Wright |
| Austin Harris | Jim Richadson | |

# Appendix D

## Church Leadership

*(Arranged in Chronological Order, from the earliest to the most recent)*

### Assistant Pastor
Richard L. Hayes (1954)

### Associate Pastor
Bro. Jones (2001)

### Brotherhood Directors

C. E. Pittman (1954)
J.B. Maddox (1955)
Clifford Sparks (1956)
James L. Sawyer (1957)
John A. Helms (1958)
J.L. Bailey (1959)
John A. Helms (1960-1961)
Clifford Sparks (1962)
C.L. Broxton (1963)
Silas Shepherd (1964)
Jimmy Bedsole (1965)
Eddie Pilgrim (1971)
Danny Herring (1972)

Louie Miller (1975)
H.E. Cordle (1976)
Louie Miller (1977-1978)
Huey Sipper (1979)
Kenneth Walden (1980)
Curtis Edwards (1981)
Clark Maddox (1982)
Huey Sipper (1983)
Robert Nicholson (1984)
Rufus McKinney
B.F. Boland
Ed Cordle
Steve Musser
Dwight Holley (1998)

### Church Clerk

J.A. Wright
J.D. Willis (1936)
John I. Jones
E.A. Sawyer (1941)
G.F. Gunter Sr. (1949 - 1951)
J.D. Willis (1952-1956)
Johnnie B. Maddox (1957-1958)

J.D. Willis (1959-1962)
Ruth Tatom (1963-1983)
Ruth McDowell (1984)
Linda Rodgers
Elaine Griswold
Magdalene Hornsby (1998)
Dot Adkison (2019)
Janice Holloway (2022-2023)

## Church Treasurer

| | |
|---|---|
| J.A. Harris (1955-1964) | Mrs. Rufus McKinney (1975-1977) |
| Cecil Clark (1965) | Ken Farris (1978-1979) |
| Leon McIntosh (1967-1971) | Mary McKinney (1980-1984) |
| Mary McKinney (1972) | Magdalene Hornsby (1998) |
| | Sharon Walker (2019-2023) |

## Deacon Chairmen

| | |
|---|---|
| J.K. Hayes (1966) | Stanley Walker (1980) |
| J.A. Harris (1971) | Rufus McKinney (1981) |
| John I. Jones (1972) | Jon Blissette (1982) |
| Brantley Williams (1975) | Huey Sipper (1983) |
| Andy Harris (1976) | Ed Cordle (1984) |
| Leon Roberts (1977) | |
| Claude Sawyer (1978-1979) | |

## Librarian

| | |
|---|---|
| Mrs. J.A. Harris (1962-1966) | Kyle Strickland (2022-2023) |

## Music Director (Choirster)

| | |
|---|---|
| Ralph H. Herring (1927) | Roy Martin (1981) |
| S.T. Jones (1956) | Jerry Griffin (1983-1984) |
| Emmette Sawyer (1956) | Mark Bower |
| E.L. Hayes (Asst. Chorister) (1956) | Mike Bright |
| Wendall Rodgers (1957) | Wendell Rodgers |
| Glen Sawyer (1958-1960) | Steven Goodson |
| Wendall Rodgers (1961-1971) | David Warren |
| Paul Conrad (1972) | Susan Enfinger (1998) |
| Andy Harris (1975) | Hal Yarbrough (2012-2016) |
| Wendall Rogers (1976) | Wiley King (2017-2022) |
| J. Barton Starr (1977) | Chuck Nelson (2022-2023) |

## Nursery Coordinator

Janice Holoway (2019-2023)

## Pianist

| | |
|---|---|
| Mrs. Dorothy Hayes (1940-1995) | Mrs. Dorothy Hayes (Asst. Pianist) (1998) |
| Miss Joan Sawyer (Asst. Pianist) (1956) | Edith King (2013-2022) |
| Susan Enfinger (1998) | Ann Reynolds (2022-2023) |

## Royal Ambassadors

W.C. Goodson (1958-1959)  
B.S. Shepard (1960-1962)

S8)  
M

## Sunday School (General Supt.)

Reben Scheffer  
J.A. Wright  
Lester Whaley  
Arch McKinnon  
J.S. Willis  
John L. Sawyer  
S.D. Fuller  
J.A. Wilkes Sr.  
J.W. Brock (1936)  
F.A. Davis (1941)  
John I. Jones (1942)  
James L. Sawyer (1949 - 1951)  
Edwin Harris (1952)  
John I. Jones (1953 -1955)  
J.L. Bailey (1956-1957)  

B.S. Shepard (1958-1960)  
W.C. Goodson (1961-1965)  
E.A. Sawyer (1966-1967)  
J.P. Moore (1969)  
Andy Harris (1971)  
Bobby Danford (1972)  
Jon Blissette (1975-1976)  
Custis Edwards (1977-1978)  
Mildred Harris (1979-1980)  
Jon Blissitte (1981)  
Glenda Roberts (1982-1983)  
James Peacock (1984)  
Leslie Griffin  
Sharon Walker  
Dwight Holley (1998)  
Kyle Strickland (2023)

## Sunday School Secretary

Sandra Locklar (2019- present)

## Training Union Director

E. A. Sawyer (1954-1958)  
John Hosier (Asst. Director) (1956)  
Joe Ben DeVane (1959-1962)  
Wendall Rodgers (1963)  
J.L. Bailey (1964)  
Glen Sawyer (1965)  
Mrs. Shirley Eades (1966)  
Mrs. Jane Wellmen (1967)  
Sonny Eads (1971)  
Eddie Pilgrim (1972)  

Huey Sipper (1975-1978)  
Louie Miller (1979)  
Harold Foster (1980)  
Ed Cordle (1981)  
Sharon Walker (1982-1983)  
Huey Sipper (1984  
Patricia Edwards  
Anges Herring  
Davis Atchison  
Dwight Holley  
William Hilyer (1998)

## W.M.U. President

Rosa B. Hunter *(The Ladies Aid)* (1905-1907)
Mrs. J.D. Willis (1927)
Mrs. S.T. Jones (1953-1954)
Mrs. L.F. Jones (1955-1957)
Mrs. J.I. Jones (1958)
Mrs. C.E. Pittman (1959)
Mrs. J.D. Willis (1960-1961)
Mrs. Joe Rodgers (1962-1963)
Mrs. J.A. Harris (1964-1965)
Mrs. C.B. Raley (1971-1972)
Mrs. J.A. Harris (1975)

Mres, Leon McIntosh (1976-1977)
Pauline Fuller (1979)
Ruby Jean Kelley (1980)
Trixie Harris (1981)
Reba Blissitte
Agnes Herring
Sharon Walker
Pat Driggers
Karen Martin (1998)
Betty Miller (2019-2023)
Midge Hogan (2023)

## Usher Coordinator

Doug Nolin (2019)
Noah Nolin (2022-2023)

## Vacation Bible School

Rev. J.H. Dykes (1950-1951)
Mrs. Claude Sawyer (1952-1955)
Mrs. Colley Pittman (1956)
Dr. John B. Johnson (1957-1958)
Mrs. J.A. Harris (Principle/superintendent) (1959-1962)

Miss Linda Jones (1962)
Mrs. J.A. Harris (1963-1964)
Rev. M.T. Gales (1965-1967)
Janice Holloway (2019-2022)
Danielle Donaldson (2023)

## Youth Leaders

Mrs. N. R. Phillips (Y.P.M.U.) (1920)
Roy Martin
Carmen Harris Bruse
Paul Copeland

Blair Andress
Jason Birchfield (1998)
Johnny Donaldson
Jennifer Pope (One Way) (2022-Current)

# Appendix E

## Letter from Rev. Mezick to the U.S. Congressman and U.S. Senators form, Alabama

Hon. Lister Hill, Senior Senator from Alabama, Washington, D. C.
Hon. John Sparkman, Senator from Alabama, Washington, D. C.
Hon. George Andrews, Congressman from Alabama, Washington, D. C.
Hon. George Grant, Congressman from Alabama, Washington, D. C.
Hon. Armistead I. Selden, Jr, Congressman from Alabama, Washington, D.C.
Hon. George Huddleston Jr, Congressman from Alabama, Washington, D. C.
Hon. Kenneth A. Roberts, Congressman from Alabama, Washington, D. C.
Hon. Albert Rains, Congressman from Alabama, Washington, D. C.
Hon. Robert E. Jones, Congressman from Alabama, Washington, D. C.
Hon. Carl Elliott, Congressman from Alabama, Washington, D. C.

We understand that super efforts are being made to get Federal tax monies made available as grants to Parochial and Private Schools. At this time we are informed that the Senate has passed a bill which would make these funds available to Parochial and Private Schools. The House had already passed a similar bill and now both bills will be sent to a Joint House-Senate Committee to thresh out the differences.

This will make millions of tax dollars available to schools of higher learning, regardless of whether they are private or religious. This bill is contrary to our beliefs concerning religion in this Country. As Baptists, we believe that Baptists should support their churches, schools and colleges, without any tax money and we feel that all other denominations should do likewise in support of their churches and schools.

The First Baptist Church of New Brockton, Alabama, wishes to go on record as being opposed to such a bill and request that you do everything in your power to prevent the passage of such a bill in our Congress.

Unanimously approved in Church Conference November 3, 1963.

FIRST BAPTIST CHURCH OF NEW BROCKTON, ALA.

Rev. C. M. Mezick, Pastor.

# Appendix F

## Documents Concerning Roland Money

New Brockton, Ala.
February 3, 1960

The Board of Deacons of The First Baptist Church of New Brockton, Alabama, in it's regular monthly meeting Tuesday evening, February 2, 1960, unanimously recommend to the church that the church authorize the property committee to have the outside woodwork and masonry painted and putty windows where needed, on the church and educational buildings. This work to be done by contract or on an hourly wage basis, this to be left to the discretion of the property committee. The work to be done at an early date convenient with the property committee.

The Board of Deacons considered a request from Chaplain James D. Sawyer, a member of our church, now serving as a Chaplain; with the Southern Baptist Convention, and after prayerful consideration, and realizing how Chaplain James D. Sawyer has consecrated his life to the ministry, unanimously recommend to the church that the church receive and welcome Roland G. Money into the full fellowship of this church.

MEMORIAL CHAPEL
Navy No. 824
% Fleet Post Office
San Francisco, California

Office of the Island Chaplain.

We, the undersigned minister and deacons, comprising an examining presbytery do certify that we have this day examined Roland G. Money, as to his experience of grace in conversion, the validity of his divine call to the ministry, his sympathy with Baptist principles and doctrines, his attitude toward the word of God, and having been satisfied with his answers do heartily recommend to the First Baptist Church, New Brockton, Alabama, that he be welcomed into their fellowship and be granted a license to preach for the purpose of preparing himself for the full gospel ministry.

January 27, 1960

/s/ James D. Sawyer, Chaplain
Chaplains Commission
Southern Baptist Convention

/s/ C. E. Williams, Deacon
Lindale Baptist Church
Corpus Christi, Texas

/s/ Claude M. Ewing, Deacon
Emmanuel Baptist Church
Corpus Christi, Texas

New Brockton, Alabama
June 7, 1960

Mr. Roland G. Money
% Memorial Chapel
Navy No. 824
% Fleet Post Office
San Francisco, California.

Dear Brother Money:

A few weeks ago, upon the recommendation of Chaplain James D. Sawyer, the First Baptist Church of New Brockton, Alabama, unanimously received you as a member and into full fellowship of the church. You were also granted a license to preach the Gospel by our church. This was also done under the recommendation of Chaplain James D. Sawyer and other members of the examining presbytery.

Until the time we may be privileged to see you personally, the Deacons of The First Baptist Church of New Brockton, Alabama, would like to take this means of extending a sincere welcome to you as a member of our church, and to express confidence in you that you will fulfill your duties as one called of God.

Our prayers will be with you and we wish for you a fruitful ministry for the Glory of God.

       Yours in Christ,

       Board of Deacons,
       First Baptist Church,
       New Brockton, Ala.

     By
       J. L. Bailey, Chairman

       C. E. Pittman, Secretary.

# Appendix G

**People Licensed, Ordained or Endorsed by the Church**

| | | |
|---|---|---|
| Richard L. Hayes | Licensed | May 30th, 1954 |
| | Ordained | August 15th, 1954 |
| James Maddox | Licensed | May 30th, 1954 |
| Elder Ellis | Licensed | January 11th, 1955 |
| James C. Mezick | Licensed | May 1955 |
| | Ordained | August 1955 |
| John Ed Sawyer | Licensed | Late 1950's |
| Jimmy D. Sawyer | Licensed | 1950's |
| | Ordained | Late 1950's |
| Roland C. Money | Licensed | February 3rd, 1960 |
| Silas Shepherd | Licensed | 1965 |
| | Ordained | 1965 |
| W. C. (Bud) Goodson | Licensed | 1965 |
| | Ordained | 1965 |
| | | |
| Miss Sarah Nell Peacock | Mission Works | May 30th, 1954 |
| Miss Peggy Helms | Mission Works | Late 1950's |
| Miss Linda Lou Jones | Mission Works | Late 1950's |

# Appendix H

## Maps

*The maps are modeled after the Alabama State Fire Maps from 1932.*

**The Location of the Brockton Old Wooden School House the home of Brockton Baptist for 1902 -1905. (Which is at the intersection of Church St. and Lee St. today.)**

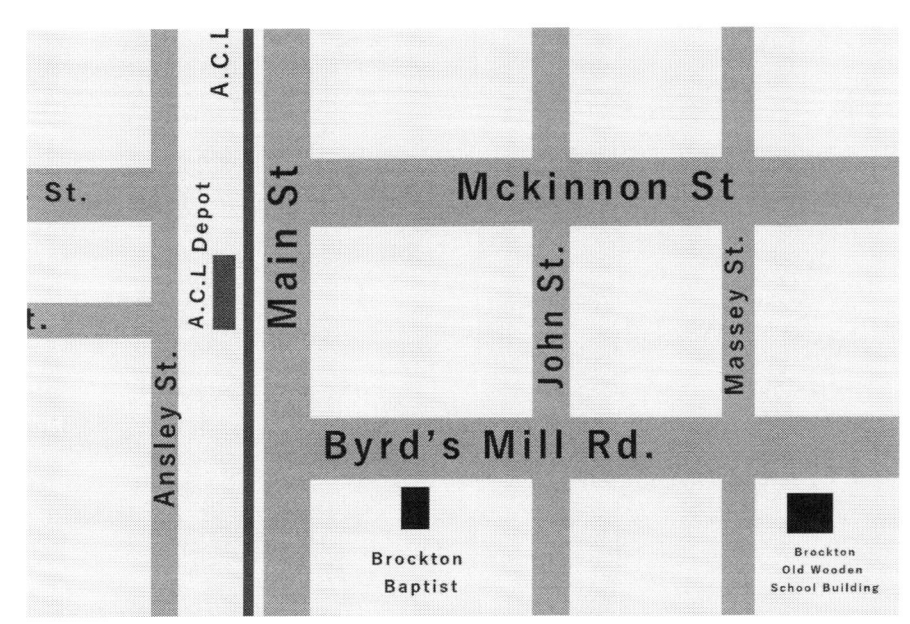

**The 1st Location of Brockton Baptist's first Building from 1905 -1905. (Which is on Church St. today.)**

**The 2nd Location of Brockton Baptist's first Building when they moved it 400 feet in 1907. (Which is at the intersection of Church St. and Lee St. today.)**

**The 2nd Building of FBC New Brockton, which was built in 1925.
(Which is the present location.)**

# Notes and References

## References for Chapter 1

### Books

The Gospel according to Matthew chapter 16

The Gospel according to Matthew chapter 28

### Images

**Page 2 (Bible inside Tower Foyer)** • 28 Sept, 2022. • (Photographer-Kyle St.Andrews)

**Page 2 (Grand Piano in Sanctuary)** • 28 Sept, 2022. • (Photographer-Kyle St.Andrews)

## References for Chapter 2

### Newspapers

The Elba Clipper by F. M. Rushing • 22 May, 1902, Thu • (page 7)(Elba, AL),
The Elba Clipper • 03 July, 1902, Thu • (Pages 2) (Elba, AL)
The People's Ledger • 03 July, 1902, Thu. •(Pages 2) (Enterprise, AL)
The People's Ledger • 17 July, 1902, Thu. • (Pages 3) (Enterprise, AL)
The Elba Clipper • 17 July, 1902, Thu. • ( page 5) (Elba, AL)

The Enterprise Ledger by Fred S. Watson • 10 Feb., 1950, Fri • (Pages 11) (Enterprise, AL),
The Elba Clipper by Fred S. Watson • 23 Feb., 1950, Thu •(Pages 7)(Elba, AL)
The Enterprise Ledger by S. D. Fuller • 8 Oct, 1954, Fri • (Sec. 2 page 1 & Sec. 2 page 4) (Enterprise, AL)
The Enterprise Ledger by Albert L. Strezier • 30 June, 1978, Fri • (page 5) (Enterprise, AL)
The Enterprise Ledger • 18 Sept, 1987, Fri • (Pages 5) (Enterprise, AL)

### Records

"First Baptist Church, New Brockton, AL Church Records", 1902-Current (these Records are stored in the Church Archives)
"History of the New Brockton First Baptist Church from 1902" (Held in the archives of the FBC New Brockton)

"First Baptist Church, New Brockton, AL Church Centennial", 1902-2002 (these Records are stored in the Church Archives & Pea River Historical Society)
"History of First Baptist Church New Brockton", 1902-1960 (these Records are stored at Pea River Historical Society)

## Books

Strozier, Albert L., • *"Coffee County Baptists, History of the Coffee County Baptist Association of Alabama and of the forty-five members of the Body"* • (1981) • (Pages 208-212)

Shoffner, Roy, • *"Go Ye Therefore…" History of the Coffee County Baptist Association 1981-1998"* • (1998) • (Pages 261-264)

History Committee • *"History of Coffee County Baptists Association, New Brockton, Alabama 1998-2002"* • (2002) • (Pages 52-53)

Watson, Fred S., • *"Coffee Grounds, A History of the Coffee County, Alabama 1941-1970"* • (1970) • (Pages 126)

## Images

**Page 6 (Rev. Robert M. Hunter)** The People's Ledger • 16 April, 1906, Mon. •(Pages 8) (Enterprise, AL) (Photographer-Unknown

**Page 6 (Old Brockton Wooden School Building)** Artist Conception • Digital Art • 16 Sep, 2023, • (Artist - KyleSt.Andrews)

**Page 10 (Pump Organ)** Artist Conception • Digital Art • 26 Sep, 2023, • (Artist - KyleSt.Andrews)

# References for Chapter 3

## Newspapers

The Elba Clipper • 04 Dec., 1902, Thu • (page 5)(Elba, AL)

The Ozark Tribune • 30 May, 1905, Tuet • (Page 8) (Ozark,AL)

The Elba Clipper • 04 Dec, 1906, Tues., • ( page 3) (Elba, AL)

The Elba Clipper • 22 Jan, 1907, Tues., • ( page 3) (Elba, AL)

The Elba Clipper • 02 April, 1907, Tues., • (pages 3 & 4) (Elba, AL)

The Ozark Tribune • 07 Dec, 1907, Sat • (Page 10) (Ozark,AL)

The Ozark Tribune • 21 Dec, 1907, Sat • (Page 9) (Ozark,AL)

The Enterprise Ledger by Fred S. Watson • 10 Feb., 1950, Fri • (Pages 11) (Enterprise, AL),

The Elba Clipper by Fred S. Watson • 23 Feb., 1950, Thu •(Pages 7)(Elba, AL)

The Enterprise Ledger by S. D. Fuller • 8 Oct, 1954, Fri • (Sec. 2 page 1 & Sec. 2 page 4) (Enterprise, AL)

The Enterprise Ledger by Albert L. Strezier • 30 June, 1978, Fri • (page 5) (Enterprise, AL)

The Enterprise Ledger • 18 Sept, 1987, Fri • (Pages 5) (Enterprise, AL)

## Records

"First Baptist Church, New Brockton, AL Church Records", 1902-Current (these Records are stored in the Church Archives)

"History of the New Brockton First Baptist Church from 1902" (Held in the archives of the FBC New Brockton)

"First Baptist Church, New Brockton, AL Church Centennial", 1902-2002 (these Records are stored in the Church Archives & Pea River Historical Society)

"History of First Baptist Church New Brockton", 1902-1960 (these Records are stored at Pea River Historical Society)

## Books

Strozier, Albert L., • *"Coffee County Baptists, History of the Coffee County Baptist Association of Alabama and of the forty-five members of the Body"* • (1981) • (Pages 208-212)

Allen, Lee N., • *"Notable Past Bright Future 1893-1993 First Baptist Church Enterprise, Alabama* • (1993) • (Pages 38-50)

## Images

**Page 12 (Rev. Robert M. Hunter)** In the Archives of Newton Baptist Church (Newton, AL) (Photographer-Unknown)
**Page 13 (Rev. Robert M. Hunter & Wife)** In the Archives of FBC Enterprise Church (Enterprise, AL) (Photographer-Unknown)

**Page 13 (Rev. D.P. Lee)** Archive from FBC Cairo, GA • Picture taken in the mid 1920's. • (Cairo, GA)
**Page 12 (First Church Building for Brockton Baptist)** Artist Conception • Digital Art • 16 Sep, 2023, • (Artist - KyleSt.Andrews)

# References for Chapter 4

## Newspapers

The Elba Clipper • 01 Dec., 1938, Thu • (Pages 1) (Elba, AL)
The Dothan Eagle • 27 Nov., 1938, Thu • (Pages 2) (Dothan, AL)
The Elba Clipper • 21 Sept., 1939,Thu. • (Pages 4) (Elba, AL)
The Enterprise Ledger • 22 Sept., 1939, Fri • (Pages 1) (Enterprise, AL
The Dothan Eagle • 28 Sept., 1939, Thu • (Pages 5) (Enterprise, AL)

The Enterprise Ledger by Fred S. Watson • 10 Feb., 1950, Fri • (Pages 11) (Enterprise, AL),
The Elba Clipper by Fred S. Watson • 23 Feb., 1950, Thu •(Pages 7)(Elba, AL)
The Enterprise Ledger by S. D. Fuller • 8 Oct, 1954, Fri • (Sec. 2 page 1 & Sec. 2 page 4) (Enterprise, AL)
The Enterprise Ledger by Albert L. Strezier • 30 June, 1978, Fri • (page 5) (Enterprise, AL)
The Enterprise Ledger • 18 Sept, 1987, Fri • (Pages 5) (Enterprise, AL)

## Records

"1936 28th annual Session Coffee County Baptist Association Minutes" (Held in the archives of the FBC New Brockton & Coffee County Baptist Association)
"First Baptist Church, New Brockton, AL Church Records", 1902-Current (these Records are stored in the Church Archives)
"History of the New Brockton First Baptist Church from 1902" (Held in the archives of the FBC New Brockton)

"First Baptist Church, New Brockton, AL Church Centennial", 1902-2002 (these Records are stored in the Church Archives & Pea River Historical Society)
"History of First Baptist Church New Brockton", 1902-1960 (these Records are stored at Pea River Historical Society)

## Books

Strozier, Albert L., • *"Coffee County Baptists, History of the Coffee County Baptist Association of Alabama and of the forty-five members of the Body"* • (1981) • (Pages 208-212)

Shoffner, Roy, • *"Go Ye Therefore…" History of the Coffee County Baptist Association 1981-1998"* • (1998) • (Page 363)

## Images

**Page 15 (Rev. Pope Lloyd Moseley)** Allen, Lee N. • *"Notable Past, Bright Future 1893-1993 FBC Enterprise, Alabama"* • (1993) • (Pages 21)

**Page 17 (Newly built New Brockton Baptist Church- 1924)** Day, Amelia Herring • *"A Quilt of Memories from a place called Home. New Brockton, Alabama"* • (2010) • (page 69) Photographer – Unknown

**Page 17 (First Baptist Church of New Brockton CornerStone – Sept. 2022)** Photographer – Kyle St.Andrews

**Page 19 (Bible School)** The Dothan Eagle • 27 June, 1937, Sun. •(Pages 8) (Dothan, AL) (Photographer-Unknown)

**Page 20 (Bible inside Tower Foyer)** • 28 Sept, 2022. • (Photographer-Kyle St.Andrews)

# References for Chapter 5

## Newspapers

The Troy Messenger • 03 April, 1941, Thu • (Pages 3) (Troy, AL)
The Dothan Eagle • 04 May, 1941, Sun • (Pages 11) (Dothan, AL)
The Troy Messenger • 06 May, 1941, Thu • (Pages 3) (Troy, AL)
The Elba Clipper • 05 Jun., 1941, Thu •(Pages 2)(Elba, AL)
The Enterprise Ledger • 15 Jun., 1945, Fri • (Pages 1) (Enterprise, AL),
The Enterprise Ledger • 26 Oct, 1945, Fri • (Pages 1) (Enterprise, AL)
The Elba Clipper • 17 Jan., 1946, Thu • (Pages 1) (Elba, AL)
The Enterprise Ledger • 18 Jan., 1946, Fri • (Pages 1) (Enterprise, AL)
The Enterprise Ledger • 25 Jan., 1946, Fri • (Pages 1) (Enterprise, AL)
The Enterprise Ledger • 14 Jun., 1946, Fri • (Pages 1) (Enterprise, AL)
The Enterprise Ledger • 05 Jul., 1946, Fri • (Pages 1) (Enterprise, AL)
The Dothan Eagle • 07 Mar, 1947, Sun • (Pages 6) (Dothan, AL)
The Enterprise Ledger • 03 Oct, 1947, Fri • (Pages 1) (Enterprise, AL)
The Enterprise Ledger • 24 Oct, 1947, Fri • (Pages 1) (Enterprise, AL)
The Enterprise Ledger • 22 April, 1948, Fri • (Pages 8) (Enterprise, AL)
The Enterprise Ledger • 23 Oct, 1948, Fri • (Pages 3) (Enterprise, AL)
The Enterprise Ledger • 08 July, 1949, Fri • (Pages 7) (Enterprise, AL)
The Dothan Eagle • 10 July, 1949, Sun • (Pages 11) (Dothan, AL)
The Montgomery Advertiser • 10 July, 1949, Sun. • (Pages 20) (Montgomery, AL)
The Montgomery Advertiser • 14 July, 1949, Thu. • (Pages 7) (Montgomery, AL)
The Enterprise Ledger • 30 Sept., 1949, Fri • (Pages 1) (Enterprise, AL)
The Enterprise Ledger • 21 Oct., 1949, Fri • (Pages 14) (Enterprise, AL)
The Dothan Eagle • 02 Oct., 1949, Sun • (Pages 13) (Dothan, AL)
The Montgomery Advertiser • 02 Oct., 1949, Sun • (Pages 2) (Montgomery, AL)
The Enterprise Ledger • 21 Oct., 1949, Fri • (Pages 14) (Enterprise, AL)
The Enterprise Ledger by Mrs. Everett Fuller • 16 Mar., 1951, Fri • (Pages 11) (Enterprise, AL)

The Enterprise Ledger • 08 Aug., 1952, Fri • (Pages 12) (Enterprise, AL)
The Enterprise Ledger • 15 Aug., 1952, Fri • (Pages 12) (Enterprise, AL)
The Enterprise Ledger by Fred S. Watson • 10 Feb., 1950, Fri • (Pages 11) (Enterprise, AL),
The Elba Clipper by Fred S. Watson • 23 Feb., 1950, Thu •(Pages 7)(Elba, AL)

The Enterprise Ledger by S. D. Fuller • 8 Oct, 1954, Fri • (Sec. 2 page 1 & Sec. 2 page 4) (Enterprise, AL)
The Enterprise Ledger by Albert L. Strezier • 30 June, 1978, Fri • (page 5) (Enterprise, AL)
The Enterprise Ledger • 18 Sept, 1987, Fri • (Pages 5) (Enterprise, AL)

## Records

"1941 33rd annual Session Coffee County Baptist Association Minutes" (Held in the archives of the FBC New Brockton & Coffee County Baptist Association)
"1942 34th annual Session Coffee County Baptist Association Minutes" (Held in the archives of the FBC New Brockton & Coffee County Baptist Association)
"1949 41st annual Session Coffee County Baptist Association Minutes" (Held in the archives of the FBC New Brockton & Coffee County Baptist Association)
"1950 42nd annual Session Coffee County Baptist Association Minutes" (Held in the archives of the FBC New Brockton & Coffee County Baptist Association)
"1951 43rd annual Session Coffee County Baptist Association Minutes" (Held in the archives of the FBC New Brockton & Coffee County Baptist Association)

"1952 44th annual Session Coffee County Baptist Association Minutes" (Held in the archives of the FBC New Brockton & Coffee County Baptist Association)
"First Baptist Church, New Brockton, AL Church Records", 1902-Current (these Records are stored in the Church Archives)
"History of the New Brockton First Baptist Church from 1902" (Held in the archives of the FBC New Brockton)
"First Baptist Church, New Brockton, AL Church Centennial", 1902-2002 (these Records are stored in the Church Archives & Pea River Historical Society)
"History of First Baptist Church New Brockton", 1902-1960 (these Records are stored at Pea River Historical Society)

## Books

Strozier, Albert L., • *"Coffee County Baptists, History of the Coffee County Baptist Association of Alabama and of the forty-five members of the Body"* • (1981) • (Pages 208-212)

Shoffner, Roy, • *"Go Ye Therefore…" History of the Coffee County Baptist Association 1981-1998"* • (1998) • (Page 364)

## Images

**Page 23 (Rev. J. H. Dykes)** The Enterprise Ledger • 23 Feb., 1951, Fri • (Pages 1) (Enterprise, AL) Photographer – Unknown

**Page 24 (Hymnal Books and Bible)** • 28 Sept, 2022. • (Photographer-Kyle St.Andrews)

# References for Chapter 6

## Newspapers

The Enterprise Ledger • 10 Apr., 1953, Fri • (Pages 5) (Enterprise, AL)
The Dothan Eagle • 12 April, 1953, Sun • (Pages 8) (Dothan, AL)
The Enterprise Ledger • 03 Jul., 1953, Fri • (Pages 2) (Enterprise, AL)
The Enterprise Ledger • 10 Jul., 1953, Fri • (Pages 1) (Enterprise, AL)
The Enterprise Ledger • 17 Jul., 1953, Fri • (Sec. 2 Pages 7) (Enterprise, AL)
The Enterprise Ledger • 31 Jul., 1953, Fri • (Pages 5) (Enterprise, AL)
The Enterprise Ledger • 19 Feb., 1954, Fri • (Pages 2) (Enterprise, AL)
The Enterprise Ledger • 07 May., 1954, Fri • (Pages 3) (Enterprise, AL)
The Enterprise Ledger • 04 Jun, 1954, Fri • (Pages 4) (Enterprise, AL)
The Enterprise Ledger • 11 Jun, 1954, Fri • (Pages 17) (Enterprise, AL)
The Enterprise Ledger • 25 Jun, 1954, Fri • (Pages 6) (Enterprise, AL)
The Enterprise Ledger • 02 Jul, 1954, Fri • (Pages 3) (Enterprise, AL)
The Enterprise Ledger • 09 Jul, 1954, Fri • (Pages 6) (Enterprise, AL)
The Enterprise Ledger • 09 Jul, 1954, Fri • (Pages 10) (Enterprise, AL)
The Enterprise Ledger • 06 Aug, 1954, Fri • (Pages 12) (Enterprise, AL)
The Enterprise Ledger • 27 Aug, 1954, Fri • (Pages 19) (Enterprise, AL)
The Enterprise Ledger • 10 Sept, 1954, Fri • (Pages 2) (Enterprise, AL)
The Enterprise Ledger • 01 Oct., 1954, Fri • (Pages 13) (Enterprise, AL)
The Enterprise Ledger • 01 Oct., 1954, Fri • (Pages 5) (Enterprise, AL)
The Enterprise Ledger • 03 Mar., 1955, Fri • (Pages 3) (Enterprise, AL)
The Enterprise Ledger • 08 Sept., 1955, Fri • (Pages 4) (Enterprise, AL)
The Enterprise Ledger • 09 Feb., 1955, Thu • (Pages 1) (Enterprise, AL)
The Enterprise Ledger • 13 Feb., 1955, Thu • (Pages 2) (Enterprise, AL)
The Enterprise Ledger by Mrs. Tom Brock • 30 Aug., 1956, Thu • (Pages 3) (Enterprise, AL)
The Dothan Eagle • 11 Nov, 1956, Sun • (Pages 22) (Dothan, AL)
The Enterprise Ledger • 17 Feb, 1957, Fri • (Pages 11) (Enterprise, AL)
The Enterprise Ledger • 16 May, 1957, Thu • (Pages 10) (Enterprise, AL)
The Enterprise Ledger • 11 Jun., 1954, Fri • (Pages 17) (Enterprise, AL)
The Enterprise Ledger • 27 Jul., 1954, Fri • (Pages 19) (Enterprise, AL)
The Enterprise Ledger • 30 Aug., 1956, Fri • (Pages 3) (Enterprise, AL)
The Enterprise Ledger by S. D. Fuller • 8 Oct, 1954, Fri • (Sec. 2 page 1 & Sec. 2 page 4) (Enterprise, AL)
The Enterprise Ledger by Albert L. Strezier • 30 June, 1978, Fri • (page 5) (Enterprise, AL)
The Enterprise Ledger • 18 Sept, 1987, Fri • (Pages 5) (Enterprise, AL)

## Records

"1953 45th annual Session Coffee County Baptist Association Minutes" (Held in the archives of the FBC New Brockton & Coffee County Baptist Association)
"1954 46th annual Session Coffee County Baptist Association Minutes" (Held in the archives of the FBC New Brockton & Coffee County Baptist Association)
"1955 47th annual Session Coffee County Baptist Association Minutes" (Held in the archives of the FBC New Brockton & Coffee County Baptist Association)
"1956 48th annual Session Coffee County Baptist Association Minutes" (Held in the archives of the FBC New Brockton & Coffee County Baptist Association)
"The Deacon's meeting Minutes 1954-1964" (Held in the archives of the FBC New Brockton)
"First Baptist Church, New Brockton, AL Church Records", 1902-Current (these Records are stored in the Church Archives)

"History of the New Brockton First Baptist Church from 1902" (Held in the archives of the FBC New Brockton)

"First Baptist Church, New Brockton, AL Church Centennial", 1902-2002 (these Records are stored in the Church Archives & Pea River Historical Society)

"History of First Baptist Church New Brockton", 1902-1960 (these Records are stored at Pea River Historical Society)

## Books

Strozier, Albert L., • *"Coffee County Baptists, History of the Coffee County Baptist Association of Alabama and of the forty-five members of the Body"* • (1981) • (Pages 208-212)

Shoffner, Roy, • *"Go Ye Therefore…" History of the Coffee County Baptist Association 1981-1998"* • (1998) • (Page 363)

## Images

**Page 26 (Rev. C. M. Mezick)** The Enterprise Ledger • 08 Aug., 1952, Fri • (Pages 12) (Enterprise, AL) Photographer – Unknown

**Page 27 (John Wallace, Mrs. Wallace & Rev. Mezick)** FBC New Brockton Archives • 25 Fed., 1954, • Photographer – Unknown

**Page 28 (Groundbreaking for the Educational Building)** The Enterprise Ledger • 19 Fed., 1954, Fri • (Pages 2) (Enterprise, AL) • Photographer – Unknown

**Page 28 (Ladies of Missionary Society)** FBC New Brockton Archives • 25 Fed., 1954, • Photographer – Unknown

**Page 28 (Deacon and Pastor)** FBC New Brockton Archives • 25 Fed., 1954, • Photographer – Unknown

**Page 29 (John Wallace and Pastor)** FBC New Brockton Archives • 25 Fed., 1954, • Photographer – Unknown

**Page 29 (Pastor Praying)** FBC New Brockton Archives • 25 Fed., 1954, • Photographer – Unknown

**Page 30 (Richard L. Hayes)** The Dothan Eagle • 28 Jul., 1957, Sun • (Pages 8) (Dothan, AL) • Photographer – Unknown

**Page 30 (James Maddox)** Entre Nous 1956 • 1956 • (Pages 98) • (Howard College Yearbook) • Photographer – Unknown

**Page 30 (Sarah Nell Peacock)** The 1955 Palladium, • 1955 • (Pages 53) • (Troy State Yearbook) • Photographer – Unknown

**Page 32 (First Baptist of New Brockton's Ed. Building Corner Stone – 2022)** Photographer – Kyle Strickland

**Page 32 (Newly built First New Brockton Baptist Ed. Building- 1954)** The Enterprise Ledger by S. D. Fuller • 8 Oct, 1954, Fri • (Sec. 2 page 1) (Enterprise, AL) Photographer – Unknown

**Page 33 (Brotherhood Dinner)** The Dothan Eagle • 11 Nov, 1956, Sun • (Pages 22) (Dothan, AL)

**Page 34 (Pulpit)** • Sept, 2022. • (Photographer-Kyle St.Andrews)

**Page 35 (James C. Mezick)** The 1956 Round-up, • 1956 • (Pages 105) • (Baylor Un. Yearbook) • Photographer – Unknown

**Page 35 (James Maddox)** Entre Nous 1955 • 1955 • (Pages 78) • (Howard College Yearbook) • Photographer – Unknown

**Page 35 (Linda Jones)** Entre Nous 1956 • 1956 • (Pages 108) • (Howard College Yearbook) • Photographer – Unknown

**Page 35 (Peggy Helms)** Entre Nous 1956 • 1956 • (Pages 108) • (Howard College Yearbook) • Photographer – Unknown

**Page 35 (Sarah Nell Peacock)** The 1957 Palladium, • 1957 • (Pages 35) • (Troy State Yearbook) • Photographer – Unknown

# References for Chapter 7

## Newspapers

The Enterprise Ledger • 17 Jul, 1958, Thu • (Pages 1) (Enterprise, AL)
The Enterprise Ledger • 09 Jul, 1960, Thu • (Pages 1) (Enterprise, AL)
The Enterprise Ledger • 11 Oct, 1960, Tues • (Pages 1) (Enterprise, AL)
The Elba Clipper • 13 Oct, 1960, Thu • (Pages 1) (Elba, AL)
The Enterprise Ledger • 23 Apr, 1963, Tues • (Pages 1) (Enterprise, AL)
The Enterprise Ledger • 04 Jun, 1963, Tues • (Pages 6) (Enterprise, AL)

The Dothan Eagle • 16 Jul, 1971, Fri • (Pages 7) (Dothan, AL)
The Dothan Eagle • 16 Mar, 1972, Thu • (Pages 36) (Dothan, AL)
The Dothan Eagle • 20 Apr, 1972, Thu • (Pages 13) (Dothan, AL)
The Enterprise Ledger by Albert L. Strezier • 30 June, 1978, Fri • (page 5) (Enterprise, AL)
The Dothan Eagle • 16 Jul, 1978, Sun • (Pages 5) (Dothan, AL)
The Enterprise Ledger • 18 Sept, 1987, Fri • (Pages 5) (Enterprise, AL)

## Records

"1957 49th annual Session Coffee County Baptist Association Minutes" (Held in the archives of the FBC New Brockton & Coffee County Baptist Association)
"1958 50th annual Session Coffee County Baptist Association Minutes" (Held in the archives of the FBC New Brockton & Coffee County Baptist Association)
"1959 51st annual Session Coffee County Baptist Association Minutes" (Held in the archives of the FBC New Brockton & Coffee County Baptist Association)
"1960 52nd annual Session Coffee County Baptist Association Minutes" (Held in the archives of the FBC New Brockton & Coffee County Baptist Association)
"1961 53rd annual Session Coffee County Baptist Association Minutes" (Held in the archives of the FBC New Brockton & Coffee County Baptist Association)
"1962 54th annual Session Coffee County Baptist Association Minutes" (Held in the archives of the FBC New Brockton & Coffee County Baptist Association)
"1963 55th annual Session Coffee County Baptist Association Minutes" (Held in the archives of the FBC New Brockton & Coffee County Baptist Association)
"1964 56th annual Session Coffee County Baptist Association Minutes" (Held in the archives of the FBC New Brockton & Coffee County Baptist Association)
"1965 57th annual Session Coffee County Baptist Association Minutes" (Held in the archives of the FBC New Brockton & Coffee County Baptist Association)
"1966 58th annual Session Coffee County Baptist Association Minutes" (Held in the archives of the FBC New Brockton & Coffee County Baptist Association)
"1967 59th annual Session Coffee County Baptist Association Minutes" (Held in the archives of the FBC New Brockton & Coffee County Baptist Association)

"1967 Coffee County Baptist Association Book of Reports" (Held in the archives of the FBC New Brockton & Coffee County Baptist Association)
"1971 63rd annual Session Coffee County Baptist Association Minutes" (Held in the archives of the FBC New Brockton & Coffee County Baptist Association)
"1972 64th annual Session Coffee County Baptist Association Minutes" (Held in the archives of the FBC New Brockton & Coffee County Baptist Association)
"1975 67th annual Session Coffee County Baptist Association Minutes" (Held in the archives of the FBC New Brockton & Coffee County Baptist Association)
"1976 68th annual Session Coffee County Baptist Association Minutes" (Held in the archives of the FBC New Brockton & Coffee County Baptist Association)
"1977 69th annual Session Coffee County Baptist Association Minutes" (Held in the archives of the FBC New Brockton & Coffee County Baptist Association)
"1978 70th annual Session Coffee County Baptist Association Minutes" (Held in the archives of the FBC New Brockton & Coffee County Baptist Association)
"1979 71th annual Session Coffee County Baptist Association Minutes" (Held in the archives of the FBC New Brockton & Coffee County Baptist Association)
"The Deacon's meeting Minutes 1954-1964" (Held in the archives of the FBC New Brockton)
"The Deacon's meeting Minutes 1964-1966" (Held in the archives of the FBC New Brockton)
"First Baptist Church, New Brockton, AL Church Records", 1902-Current (these Records are stored in the Church Archives)

"History of the New Brockton First Baptist Church from 1902" (Held in the archives of the FBC New Brockton)

"First Baptist Church, New Brockton, AL Church Centennial", 1902-2002 (these Records are stored in the Church Archives & Pea River Historical Society)

"History of First Baptist Church New Brockton", 1902-1960 (these Records are stored at Pea River Historical Society)

## Books

Strozier, Albert L., • *"Coffee County Baptists, History of the Coffee County Baptist Association of Alabama and of the forty-five members of the Body"* • (1981) • (Pages 208-212)

Shoffner, Roy, • *"Go Ye Therefore…" History of the Coffee County Baptist Association 1981-1998"* • (1998) • (Page 363)

## Images

**Page 36 (John D. Johnson)** The Alexander City Outlook • 04 Mar, 1955, Frin • (page 1) (Alexander City, AL) Photographer – Unknown

**Page 38 (VBS)** The Enterprise Ledger • 04 Jun, 1963, Tues • (Pages 6) (Enterprise, AL) Photographer – Tri-State Studio

**Page 38 (FBC New Brockton 1960)** Watson, Fred, • *"Coffee Grounds" A history of Coffee County, Alabama 1841 - 1970"* • (1970) • Photographer – Fred Watson

**Page 41 (Joyce and Colbert Croft)** The Dothan Eagle • 18 Jul, 1976, Sun • (page 6) (Dothan, AL) Photographer – Unknown

**Page 42 (Mr. & Mrs. David Richburg, Marica and James David II)** The Enterprise Ledger by Albert L. Strezier • 30 June, 1978, Fri • (page 5) (Enterprise, AL) Photographer – Unknown

**Page 42 (FBC Deacon 1978)** The Enterprise Ledger by Albert L. Strezier • 30 June, 1978, Fri • (page 5) (Enterprise, AL) Photographer – Unknown

**Page 43 (David Richburg)** Shoffner, Roy, • *"Go Ye Therefore…" History of the Coffee County Baptist Association 1981-1998"* • (1998) • (Page 77) • Photographer – Unknown

# References for Chapter 8

## Newspapers

The Enterprise Ledger • 18 Sept, 1987, Fri • (Pages 5) (Enterprise, AL)

The Dothan Eagle • 13 Apr, 1996, Sat • (Pages 27) (Dothan, AL)

The Dothan Eagle • 20 Apr, 1996, Sat • (Pages 27) (Dothan, AL)

The Dothan Eagle • 27 Apr, 1996, Sat • (Pages 27) (Dothan, AL)

The Dothan Eagle • 04 May, 1996, Sat • (Pages 27) (Dothan, AL)

## Records

"1980 72nd annual Session Coffee County Baptist Association Minutes" (Held in the archives of the FBC New Brockton & Coffee County Baptist Association)

"1981 73rd annual Session Coffee County Baptist Association Minutes" (Held in the archives of the FBC New Brockton & Coffee County Baptist Association)

"1982 74th annual Session Coffee County Baptist Association Minutes" (Held in the archives of the FBC New Brockton & Coffee County Baptist Association)
"1983 75th annual Session Coffee County Baptist Association Minutes" (Held in the archives of the FBC New Brockton & Coffee County Baptist Association)
"1984 76th annual Session Coffee County Baptist Association Minutes" (Held in the archives of the FBC New Brockton & Coffee County Baptist Association)
"The Deacon's meeting Minutes 1999-2020" (Held in the archives of the FBC New Brockton)

"First Baptist Church, New Brockton, AL Church Records", 1902-Current (these Records are stored in the Church Archives)
"History of the New Brockton First Baptist Church from 1902" (Held in the archives of the FBC New Brockton)
"First Baptist Church, New Brockton, AL Church Centennial", 1902-2002 (these Records are stored in the Church Archives & Pea River Historical Society)

## Books

Strozier, Albert L., • *"Coffee County Baptists, History of the Coffee County Baptist Association of Alabama and of the forty-five members of the Body"* • (1981) • (Pages 208-212)
Shoffner, Roy, • *"Go Ye Therefore..." History of the Coffee County Baptist Association 1981-1998"* • (1998) • (Page 363)

History Committee • *"History of Coffee County Baptists Association, New Brockton, Alabama 1998-2002"* • (2002) • (Pages 52-53)

## Images

**Page 44 (Rev. Rex Henderson)** Strozier, Albert L., • *"Coffee County Baptists, History of the Coffee County Baptist Association of Alabama and of the forty-five members of the Body"* • (1981) • (Page 208) • Photographer – Unknown
**Page 45 (First Baptist of New Brockton before Renovation – 1987)** The Enterprise Ledger • 18 Sept, 1987, Fri • (Pages 5) (Enterprise, AL) Photographer – Unknown
**Page 46 (First Baptist of New Brockton after Renovation – 1987)** The Enterprise Ledger • 18 Sept, 1987, Fri • (Pages 5) (Enterprise, AL) Photographer – Unknown

**Page 46 (Sanctuary)** The Enterprise Ledger • 18 Sept, 1987, Fri • (Pages 5) (Enterprise, AL)
**Page 47 (Rev. Bob Barr)** Shoffner, Roy, • *"Go Ye Therefore..." History of the Coffee County Baptist Association 1981-1998"* • (1998) • (Page 261) Photographer – Unknown
**Page 48 (FBC 2000)** • Coffee County Baptists Association Website • (Church Directory) • (coffeebaptist.com) • Photographer – Unknown

# References for Chapter 9

## Newspapers
The Alabama Baptist • 3 Sept, 2009, • (thealabamabaptist.org)

## Records

"The Deacon's meeting Minutes 1999-2020" (Held in the archives of the FBC New Brockton)
"First Baptist Church, New Brockton, AL Church Records", 1902-Current (these Records are stored in the Church Archives)
"History of the New Brockton First Baptist Church from 1902" (Held in the archives of the FBC New Brockton)

"First Baptist Church, New Brockton, AL Church Centennial", 1902-2002 (these Records are stored in the Church Archives & Pea River Historical Society)

## Books

Strozier, Albert L., • *"Coffee County Baptists, History of the Coffee County Baptist Association of Alabama and of the forty-five members of the Body"* • (1981) • (Pages 208-212)
Shoffner, Roy, • *"Go Ye Therefore..." History of the Coffee County Baptist Association 1981-1998"* • (1998) • (Page 363)

History Committee • *"History of Coffee County Baptists Association, New Brockton, Alabama 1998-2002"* • (2002) • (Pages 52-53)

## Images

**Page 50 (Rev. Chad Hixson)** • History Committee • *"History of Coffee County Baptists Association, New Brockton, Alabama 1998-2002"* • (2002) • (Pages 52) • Photographer – Unknown
**Page 51 (Rev. Slade Stinson)** • Coffee County Baptists Association Website • (Pastor Directory) • (coffeebaptist.com) • Photographer – Unknown

**Page 52 (FBC NB 2000)** • 28 Sept, 2022. • (Photographer-Kyle St.Andrews)
**Page 52 (FBC NB 2000)** • 28 Sept, 2022. • (Photographer-Kyle St.Andrews)

# References for Chapter 10

## Newspapers

The Elba Clipper • 23 Feb, 2012, • (elba-clipper.com)
The Alabama Baptist • 28 Feb, 2013, • (thealabamabaptist.org)
The Enterprise Ledger • 28 Feb, 2013, Rhu • (Pages 2) (Enterprise, AL)
The Enterprise Ledger • 03 Mar, 2013, Sun • (Pages 5) (Enterprise, AL)
The Dothan Eagle • 03 Mar, 2013, Sun • (Pages 4) (Dothan, AL)
The Dothan Eagle • 06 Mar, 2013, Wed • (Pages 22) (Dothan, AL)
The Enterprise Ledger • 08 Mar, 2013, Fri • (Pages 2) (Enterprise, AL)
The Enterprise Ledger • 10 Mar, 2013, Sun • (Pages 2) (Enterprise, AL)
The Dothan Eagle • 09 Mar, 2014, Sun • (Pages 8) (Dothan, AL)
The Alabama Baptist • 13 Mar, 2014, • (thealabamabaptist.org)
The Dothan Eagle • 16 Mar, 2014, Sun • (Pages 9) (Dothan, AL)
The Dothan Eagle • 15 Mar, 2017, Wed • (Pages 22) (Dothan, AL)
The Enterprise Leader • 15 Mar, 2017, Wed • (Pages 3) (Enterprise, AL)
The Alabama Baptist • 17 Mar, 2017, • (thealabamabaptist.org)
The Alabama Baptist • 14 Feb, 2018, • (thealabamabaptist.org)
The Elba Clipper • 15 Feb, 2018, • (elba-clipper.com)
The Dothan Eagle • 21 Feb, 2018, Wed • (Pages 22) (Dothan, AL)
The Alabama Baptist • 06 Feb, 2019, • (thealabamabaptist.org)
The Montgomery Advertiser • 28 Mar, 2020, Sun • (Pages A1) (Montgomery, AL)
The Montgomery Advertiser • 04 Apr, 2020, Sun • (Pages A1 & A2) (Montgomery, AL)

## Records

"The Deacon's meeting Minutes 1999-2020" (Held in the archives of the FBC New Brockton)

"First Baptist Church, New Brockton, AL Church Records", 1902-Current (these Records are stored in the Church Archives)

## Images

**Page 53 (Rev. Nathan Sims)** The Alabama Baptist • 04 Sep, 2020, • (thealabamabaptist.org)
Photographer – Unknown

**Page 54 (Wiley & Edith King)** The Alabama Baptist • 04 Sep, 2020, • (thealabamabaptist.org)
Photographer – Unknown

**Page 57 (FBC NB 2000)** • 28 Sept, 2022. • (Photographer-Kyle St.Andrews)

# References for Chapter 11

## Newspapers

The Elba Clipper • 06 Oct, 2022, • (elba-clipper.com)

## Records

"First Baptist Church, New Brockton, AL Church Records", 1902-Current (these Records are stored in the Church Archives)

## Images

**Page 58 (Rev. Pope on the Christmas Float)** • 03 Dec, 2022. • (Photographer-Kyle St.Andrews)
**Page 58 (The Christmas Float)** • 03 Dec, 2022. • (Photographer-Kyle St.Andrews)
**Page 59 (Harmony Cantata)** • 04 Dec, 2022. • (Photographer-Kyle St.Andrews)
**Page 59 (One way logo)** in the archives of FBC • (Photographer-Unknown)
**Page 60 (Damascus Cantata)** • 14 Dec, 2022. • (Photographer-Kyle St.Andrews)

**Page 61 (MFuge)** • 05 Jun, 2023. • (Photographer-Unknown)
**Page 62 (2023 VBS)** • (Photographer-Kyle St.Andrews)
**Page 63 (2023 VBS)** • (Photographer-Kyle St.Andrews)
**Page 64 (Rev. Pope & Jennife Pope)** • (Photographer-Unknown)

# Appendix

## Newspapers-

The Elba Clipper • 10 Oct., 1911, Tus • (Pages 1) (Elba, AL),
The Elba Clipper • 14 Jul., 1927, Thu • (Pages 1) (Elba, AL),
The Elba Clipper • 24 Nov., 1927, Thu • (Pages 1) (Elba, AL),
The Enterprise Ledger by Fred S. Watson • 10 Feb., 1950, Fri • (Pages 11) (Enterprise, AL),
The Elba Clipper by Fred S. Watson • 23 Feb., 1950, Thu •(Pages 7)(Elba, AL)
The Enterprise Ledger • 04 Dec., 1953, Fri • (Pages 20) (Enterprise, AL),

The Enterprise Ledger by S. D. Fuller • 8 Oct, 1954, Fri • (Sec. 2 page 1 & Sec. 2 page 4) (Enterprise, AL)
The Enterprise Ledger by Mrs. Tom Brock • 06 Oct., 1955, Thu • (Pages 15) (Enterprise, AL),
The Enterprise Ledger by Albert L. Strezier • 30 June, 1978, Fri • (page 5) (Enterprise, AL)
The Enterprise Ledger • 18 Sept, 1987, Fri • (Pages 5) (Enterprise, AL)
The Dothan Eagle • 02 Apr., 1997, Wed • (Pages 11) (Dothan, AL),

# Records

"1936 28th annual Session Coffee County Baptist Association Minutes" (Held in the archives of the FBC New Brockton & Coffee County Baptist Association)
"1941 33rd annual Session Coffee County Baptist Association Minutes" (Held in the archives of the FBC New Brockton & Coffee County Baptist Association)
"1942 34th annual Session Coffee County Baptist Association Minutes" (Held in the archives of the FBC New Brockton & Coffee County Baptist Association)
"1949 41st annual Session Coffee County Baptist Association Minutes" (Held in the archives of the FBC New Brockton & Coffee County Baptist Association)
"1950 42nd annual Session Coffee County Baptist Association Minutes" (Held in the archives of the FBC New Brockton & Coffee County Baptist Association)
"1951 43rd annual Session Coffee County Baptist Association Minutes" (Held in the archives of the FBC New Brockton & Coffee County Baptist Association)
"1952 44th annual Session Coffee County Baptist Association Minutes" (Held in the archives of the FBC New Brockton & Coffee County Baptist Association)
"1953 45th annual Session Coffee County Baptist Association Minutes" (Held in the archives of the FBC New Brockton & Coffee County Baptist Association)
"1954 46th annual Session Coffee County Baptist Association Minutes" (Held in the archives of the FBC New Brockton & Coffee County Baptist Association)
"1955 47th annual Session Coffee County Baptist Association Minutes" (Held in the archives of the FBC New Brockton & Coffee County Baptist Association)
"1956 48th annual Session Coffee County Baptist Association Minutes" (Held in the archives of the FBC New Brockton & Coffee County Baptist Association)
"1957 49th annual Session Coffee County Baptist Association Minutes" (Held in the archives of the FBC New Brockton & Coffee County Baptist Association)
"1958 50th annual Session Coffee County Baptist Association Minutes" (Held in the archives of the FBC New Brockton & Coffee County Baptist Association)
"1959 51st annual Session Coffee County Baptist Association Minutes" (Held in the archives of the FBC New Brockton & Coffee County Baptist Association)
"1960 52nd annual Session Coffee County Baptist Association Minutes" (Held in the archives of the FBC New Brockton & Coffee County Baptist Association)
"1961 53rd annual Session Coffee County Baptist Association Minutes" (Held in the archives of the FBC New Brockton & Coffee County Baptist Association)
"1962 54th annual Session Coffee County Baptist Association Minutes" (Held in the archives of the FBC New Brockton & Coffee County Baptist Association)
"1963 55th annual Session Coffee County Baptist Association Minutes" (Held in the archives of the FBC New Brockton & Coffee County Baptist Association)
"1964 56th annual Session Coffee County Baptist Association Minutes" (Held in the archives of the FBC New Brockton & Coffee County Baptist Association)
"1965 57th annual Session Coffee County Baptist Association Minutes" (Held in the archives of the FBC New Brockton & Coffee County Baptist Association)
"1966 58th annual Session Coffee County Baptist Association Minutes" (Held in the archives of the FBC New Brockton & Coffee County Baptist Association)
"1967 59th annual Session Coffee County Baptist Association Minutes" (Held in the archives of the FBC New Brockton & Coffee County Baptist Association)

"1967 Coffee County Baptist Association Book of Reports" (Held in the archives of the FBC New Brockton & Coffee County Baptist Association)

"1971 63rd annual Session Coffee County Baptist Association Minutes" (Held in the archives of the FBC New Brockton & Coffee County Baptist Association)

"1972 64th annual Session Coffee County Baptist Association Minutes" (Held in the archives of the FBC New Brockton & Coffee County Baptist Association)

"1975 67th annual Session Coffee County Baptist Association Minutes" (Held in the archives of the FBC New Brockton & Coffee County Baptist Association)

"1976 68th annual Session Coffee County Baptist Association Minutes" (Held in the archives of the FBC New Brockton & Coffee County Baptist Association)

"1977 69th annual Session Coffee County Baptist Association Minutes" (Held in the archives of the FBC New Brockton & Coffee County Baptist Association)

"1978 70th annual Session Coffee County Baptist Association Minutes" (Held in the archives of the FBC New Brockton & Coffee County Baptist Association)

"1979 71st annual Session Coffee County Baptist Association Minutes" (Held in the archives of the FBC New Brockton & Coffee County Baptist Association)

"1980 72nd annual Session Coffee County Baptist Association Minutes" (Held in the archives of the FBC New Brockton & Coffee County Baptist Association)

"1981 73rd annual Session Coffee County Baptist Association Minutes" (Held in the archives of the FBC New Brockton & Coffee County Baptist Association)

"1982 74th annual Session Coffee County Baptist Association Minutes" (Held in the archives of the FBC New Brockton & Coffee County Baptist Association)

"1983 75th annual Session Coffee County Baptist Association Minutes" (Held in the archives of the FBC New Brockton & Coffee County Baptist Association)

"1984 76th annual Session Coffee County Baptist Association Minutes" (Held in the archives of the FBC New Brockton & Coffee County Baptist Association)

"The Deacon's meeting Minutes 1954-1964" (Held in the archives of the FBC New Brockton)

"The Deacon's meeting Minutes 1964-1966" (Held in the archives of the FBC New Brockton)

"The Deacon's meeting Minutes 1999-2020" (Held in the archives of the FBC New Brockton)

"History of the New Brockton First Baptist Church from 1902" (Held in the archives of the FBC New Brockton)

"First Baptist Church, New Brockton, AL Church Centennial", 1902-2002 (these Records are stored in the Church Archives & Pea River Historical Society)

"History of First Baptist Church New Brockton", 1902-1960 (these Records are stored at Pea River Historical Society)

## Books

Strozier, Albert L., • *"Coffee County Baptists, History of the Coffee County Baptist Association of Alabama and of the forty-five members of the Body"* • (1981) • (Pages 208-212)

Shoffner, Roy, • *"Go Ye Therefore..." History of the Coffee County Baptist Association 1981-1998"* • (1998) • (Page 363)

# INDEX

### -A-

Adams, Leon (Rev.) - 56, 67
Air National Guard - 40
African American Missionary - 31

**Alabama,**
  Alabaster - 36
  Baldwin Co. - 42
  Bullock Co. - 7
  Birmingham - 3, 22, 55
  (West) Blockton - 10, 14
  (New) Brockton
    City Hall - 27
    Christmas Parade - 58
      (Picture) - 58
    Elementary School - 66
    Fall Festival - *(See Light the Night)*
    Fire - 10
    Founding - 4
    High School - 19, 66
      (Picture) - 19
    Name Change - 10-11
    Middle School - 66
    Old Wooden School House - 5-6
      (Picture) - 6
    Streets
      Byrd's Mill rd. - 5, 9, 11
      Church St. - 5, 9, 11
      Lee St. - 5, 11, 17, 55
      McKinnon St. - 17, 18
      Massy St. - 5, 11, 17
      Main St. - 18
    Theater - 27
    Warehouse - 27
  Brundidge - 24
  Butler - 68
  Clanton - 55, 56
  Clintonville - 16
  Dothan - 24, 33, 40, 54, 56
  Deatsville - 21
  Elba - 3-4, 9, 12, 14, 15, 16, 17, 19, 21, 23, 24, 31, 33
  Enterprise - 3-4, 8, 9, 11, 12, 15, 18, 31, 37, 40, 55, 56
  Fort Payne - 55
  Fort Rucker - 36
  Gantt - 55
  Goodman - 9, 18, 48
  Gurley - 16
  Hartford - 18, 22, 54
  Houston Co. - 44
  Jack - 8, 22, 23
  Kinston - 45
  Level Plains - 40
  Luverne - 21
  Montgomery - 16, 40
  Newton - 7, 16
  Newville - 16
  Opelika - 32
  Opp - 32
  Ozark - 7
  Pike Co. - 47
  Prattville - 40
  Troy - 14
  Union Springs - 8
  Warrior - 33

*Alabama Baptist* (Newspaper) - 25
Alabama Baptist State Convention - 15, 45, 49
Alabama Historical Commission - 49
Ammerman, Claude T. (Rev.) - 24
Atchison, David (Rev.) - 46

Atlantic Coast Line R.R. - 9, 11

## -B-

Bailey, Ernest (Dr.) - 61
Baker, A. W (Rev.) - 20
Banquet
    Brotherhood - 33
        (Picture) - 33
    Valentine's Day - 61
Baptist Collegiate Institute (Newton) - 16
Baptist Young People's Union - 16
Baptism - 5,15
Baptize - 2, 5, 7, 8,9, 18, 24, 25, 33, 38, 39, 40, 63
Barr, Robert (Bob) (Rev.) - 47-48
    (Picture) - 47
Beasley, H.W. (Rev.) - 20
Bentley, C.J. -15
Bentley, Shawn (Rev.) - 55
Bevis, R.D. (Rev.) - 16
Bible School for Children -19
    (Picture) - 19
Blessing Box -63-64, 66, 73
Blissitte, Jon -49, 63, 70
Blissitte, Reba - 71
Brock Country Store - 3
Brock, Hugh - 3, 5, 8, 9
Brock, J.A. (Mrs.) - 27
Brock, Jessie - 5,
Brooks, E.D. - 12
Brown, Lee - 70
Broxton, LaRue - 38
    (Picture) - 38
Bruce, Ralph - 42
    (Picture) - 42
Brunson, Bertie -5
Brunson, Bessie. -5
Brunson, Collie. -5
Brunson, E.G. - 4, 8, 70
Brunson, Ed. -5
Brush Arbor - 4
Bush, W. M.(Rev.) - 18-19

## -C-

Caesarea Philippi -1
Cantata
    Christmas - *(see Christmas Cantata)*
    Easter - *(see Easter Cantata)*
Children's Worship -46
Christmas Cantata - 59, 60
    (Picture) - 59, 60

**Church (FBC New Brockton)**
    100 year - Centennial Celebration - 49
    Air Conditioning - 37
    Baptism Service - 5
    Budget - 23, 25
    Bulletins - 23
    Building Committee - 8, 17
    Chimes (Bell) - 24
    Choir - 6, 71
    Cornerstone - 17, 31-32
        (Picture) - 17, 32
    Educational Building - 27-31,
        (Picture) - 31
    Fellowship Hall - 45
    First Church Building - 8-9
        (Picture) - 12
    Founding Members - 4-5
    Homecoming Service - 40
    Incorporation - 44
    Library - 36
    Organ - 10
        (Picture) - 10
    Pastorium - 18, 55
    Pews - 14, 23
    Pulpit - 25, 67
        (Picture) - 34
    Renovation - 16, 45-46
        (Picture) - 45-46
    Repairs to the Church - 16
    Sanctuary - 5, 46, 54
        (Picture) - 46
    Second Church Building - 16-17
        (Picture) - 16, 38

Secretarial equipment - 36
Social Media - 57
Van - 47, 48
Website - 57
Windows - 54

**Churches (Other)**
Bethany Baptist - 3, 24, 37, 57
Bethel Baptist (Newton) - 7, 71
Calvary Baptist (Butler) - 68
Calvary Baptist (Enterprise) - 8, 11, 40, 55, 56
Calvary Baptist (Texas) - 63-64
Church on Boll Weevil Circle - 56
Clintonville Primitive Baptist - 16
Coffee County Cowboy Church - 57
Connect Church (AG) - 57
Cool Springs Baptist - 18
County Line Baptist (Dothan Hwy) -24, 33
David St. Baptist (Greenville, SC) - 42
Daleville Baptist - 9
Damascus Baptist - 7, 8, 9, 24, 57, 60, 65
    (Picture) - 60
Derita Baptist (North Carolina) - 37
FBC Avondale - 3
FBC Brundidge - 24
FBC Elba - 4, 9, 14, 15
FBC Enterprise - 4, 9, 18, 23
FBC Gantt - 55
FBC Gurley - 16
FBC Fort Payne - 55
FBC Level Plains -40
FBC Kinston - 45
FBC Opelika - 32
FBC Opp - 32
FBC Robertsdale - 42
FBC Troy - 14, 24
First Methodist of New Brockton - 32
Goodman Baptist - 18, 40, 48
Hartford Baptist - 54
Harmony Baptist - 59, 61, 65
    (Picture) - 59
Hebron Baptist - 22

Indian Creek Baptist (Bullock Co.) - 7, 8
Ino Baptist - 47
Inverness Baptist (Union Springs) - 8
Lakeside Baptist (Birmingham) -55
Luverne Baptist - 21
Mt. Gilead Baptist (Dothan) - 56
Mt. Olive Baptist - 19, 33
Mt. Olive Baptist (Pensacola, FL)- 48
Mt. Pleasant Baptist - 31, 37
Mt. Zion Baptist - 65
New Ebenezer Baptist - 17
New Home Baptist - 56
New Hope Baptist (Jack) - 8, 23
North Side Baptist (Georgia) - 37
Park Ave. Baptist (Elba) - 31
Park Ave. Baptist (Enterprise) - 23, 31, 56
Poplar Springs Baptist - 31
Oenaville Baptist (Texas) - 32
Ozark Baptist- 7
Samson Baptist - 19
Siluria Baptist - 36
Southside Baptist (Dothan) - 54
Southside Baptist (Montgomery) - 40
St. Luke Methodist - 40
Victoria Baptist - 8
West Gate AG (Enterprise) - 40
Westview Baptist (Enterprise) - 37

Clark, Kay - 56, 67
Cobb, Kevin - 54
Coffee County Baptist Association - 11, 12, 15, 16, 17,18, 19, 20, 21, 22, 23, 24, 37, 39, 40, 42, 45, 49, 67
Coffee Co. Baptist Women's Missionary Society - 39
Coffee County Missionary Baptist Preachers Society - 21
Coffee County Baptist Sunday School Convention - 22
Confederate Veteran - 7
Cox, Tim (Dr.) - 22
COVID-19 - 56
Crabtree, H.L. - 17
Croft, Colbert (Rev.) -40-41, 49
    (Picture) - 41

Croft, Joyce - 41, 49
    (Picture) - 41
Crumpler, J.G. -17
Crumpton, W.B. (Dr.) - 15
Colley Pittman Mere Co. (Business) -27
Cox E.E. - 22
Cox, Tim (Dr.) - 55

## -D-

Deacon - 9, 14, 27, 37, 42, 56, 70
    Emeritus - 63
    (Picture) - 27, 28, 29, 42
Dean, Pearl - 5
Diffey, Chris - 55
Donaldson, Danielle - 62, 72
Donaldson, Johnny - 61
Donaldson, Scott (Rev.) - 65
Friggers. Pat - 71
Driver, Ronnie - 40
Dykes, J. Hollan (Rev.) - 23-24, 72
    (Picture) - 24

## -E-

Eady, James W. (Rev.) - 32, 37
Easter Cantata - 61
Elijah (Prophet) - 1
Ellis, Eldrid (Rev.) - 32, 34
Enterprise State Jr. College (ESJC) - 40
Evangelist - 8, 26, 36, 37, 40, 42, 51, 54, 55, 56
Evangelistic Crusade - 24

## -F-

Family Night - 67
First Baptist Church of New Brockton, Inc. - 44
Fleming, Frank J. (Rev) - 21

**Florida**
    Pensacola - 48

Fort Rucker "Meddacs" - 40
Fort Rucker "Smoke & Rockets" - 40
Freese, Phil - 61, 73
Fuller, Pauline - 71
Fuller, S.D. -17, 18, 27, 70

## -G-

Gable L.A. Jr. (Rev.) - 26, 37
Garrett, Lester (Rev.) - 40
Gales, M.T. (Rev.) - 39

**Georgia**
    Milledgeville - 37

GOD - 1-2, 15, 22, 26, 33, 65, 66, 67, 72, 74-75
Goodson, W.C. "Bud" (Rev.) - 39
Gospel - 2, 5, 31, 32, 37, 39, 65, 68, 73, 74-75
Graham, Don (Evangelist) - 55, 56
Granger, John (Dr.) - 48, 49, 56, 65, 67
Great Spiritual Awakening - 26-34
Griffin, Jerry - 71
Growth Meeting - 58

## -H-

Hand Up - 66
Hargrove, Harry W. (Rev.) - 24
Hargrove M.M. (Rev.) - 36
Harper, W.B - 4, 8
Harris, Austin - 42
    (Picture) - 42
Harris, J.A. - 23
Harris J.A. (Mrs.) - 38
    (Picture) - 38
Harris, Trixie - 71
Harrison, Vicky - 61. 68
Haw Ridge Baptist Association - 11
Hayes, J.K. - 42

108

(Picture) - 42
Hayes, Patricia - 38
    (Picture) - 38
Hayes, Richard L. "Dick" (Rev.) - 30-31, 34, 37
    (Picture) - 30
Helms, Lloyd - 54
Helms, Peggy - 34
    (Picture) - 35
Henderson, Rex Edmon (Rev.) - 44-46
    (Picture) - 44
Herring, Ralph - 71
Hixson, Chad (Rev.) - 50, 53
    (Picture) - 50
Hixson. Eric - 51
Hogan, Chuck - 61, 68, 73
Hogan, Midge - 63, 72
Hogg, George -42
    (Picture) - 42
Holidays
    Christmas - 58--60
    Christmas Eve - 60
    Easter - 61
    Thanksgiving Day - 10
    Valentine's Day - 61
Holloway, Janice - 56, 72
Hood, "Buddy" (Rev.) - 54
Howard College- 31-32
Howard Extension Center (FBC NB) -31-32
**HOLY SPIRIT (SPIRIT of GOD)** -2, 4, 15, 26, 68
Hudson, John N. (Chaplin) - 36
Hunter, R.M. (Rev) - 3-6, 9-11, 18
    (Picture) - 6, 13
Hunter, Rosa B. - 9
    (Picture) - 13

### -I-

Ikner, Alfred (Rev.) - 40
Ivey, Kay (Gov.) - 56

### -J-

**JESUS CHRIST** - 1-2, 4, 7, 65, 66, 68, 72, 73, 74-75
Jeremiah (Prophet) - 1
John The Baptist - 1
Johnson, Henry (Rev.) - 49
Johnson, John B.(Dr.) -33-36, 72
    (Picture) - 36
Johnson, J.S. (Rev.) -16-17
Joint Revival Service - *(see Revival)*
Jones, Howard (Rev.) - 42
Jones, J.T. - 17
Jones, Linda Lou - 34, 72
    (Picture) - 35
Jones, Q.P. - 37
Jones, S.T. - 27, 71
Jones,. J. W. (Rev.) - 21-22
Justice, B. R. (Dr.) - 23

### -K-

Kelly, J.D. (Rev.) -40
Kendrick, Paul (Rev.) - 39
King, Edith - 54
    (Picture) - 54
King, Wiley - 55
    (Picture) - 54
King, Mack (Rev.) - 46

### -L-

Ladies Aid Group - (See W.M.U.)
Ladies of Missionary Society - 28
    (Picture) - 28
Lambert, Patricia - 38
    (Picture) - 38
Langham, J.J. (Professor) - 17
Layman's Revival - 22
Lee, Dallas P (Rev) - 14
    (Picture) - 13
Lester, J.W. Lester (Rev) - 31
Licensed - 7, 30, 32, 34, 37, 39
Light the Night - 57
Lindsey, John F. (Rev.) - 37
Lions Club -40

Locklar, Pat -38
    (Picture) - 38
Loftin, J.M. - 14-15
Lord's Supper - 61
Lloyd, Eugene (Rev.) - 42
Lowery, J.A. (Dr.) - 16

## -M-

McCree, Ida - 5
McGee, Berchie - 5
McKinney, Rufus - 42
    (Picture) - 42
McWhirter, Frank Carswell (Rev.) -39
Maddox, J.B. - 27
Maddox, James - 30, 34
    (Picture) - 30, 35
Matthews, Critten Lingston (Rev) - 7-9
Marsh, Florence - 5
Marsh, Malissa - 5
Martz,. A. O. (Rev.) - 31
May, Ken (Rev.) - 47
Men's Brotherhood - 18, 70-7, 73
Men's Ministry - 61, 63-64, 66, 73
Mezick, Clarence M. (Rev.) - 24-33, 37-38
    (Picture) - 26, 27-29, 38
Mezick, James C. (Rev.) - 32, 34
    (Picture) - 35
MFUGE - 61
    (Picture) - 61-62
Miller, Betty -72
Missionary - 12, 15, 23. 30, 33, 34
Missionary Baptist - 4, 21
Moderator - 23, 37, 42
Money, Roland C. - 37
Moore, Carlton (Rev.) - 48
Moore, Jan - 57
Moore, J.M. (Mrs.) - 5
Moore, J.M. (Rev.) - 3-4
Moore, Obe H. - 3,
Moore, Winston W. - 9
Moseley, Pope Lloyd (Rev.) - 15
    (Picture) - 15

Mt. Hermon - 1
M.U.D. Ministries - 51

## -N-

Nall, L.A. (Rev.) -16
Nelson, Chuck - 57, 61, 68, 71, 73
Nolin, Dale - 61, 73
Nolin, Doug - 56, 63, 70
Nolin, Noah -61, 73

**North Carolina**
    Charlotte - 26, 37

## -O-

One Way Student Ministries - 59, 61-62
    (Picture) - 59, 61-62
Ordained - 7, 32, 34, 37

## -P-

Parade - 58
    (Picture) - 58
Pate, E.S. (Rev.) - 21
Pea River Baptist Association - 8, 11
Peacock, Jimmy - 42
    (Picture) - 42
Peacock, Sarah Nell - 30, 34
    (Picture) - 30, 35
Peter (Disciple) - 1
Phillips, J.P. - 8
Phillips, N.R. (Mrs.) - 16
Polio Threat - 22
Pope, Ben - 73
Pope, Jennifer - 59, 68, 73
    (Picture) - 61, 62, 64
Pope, Stephen (Rev.) - 57-64, 65-66, 68, 73
    (Picture) - 58, 61, 62, 64
Potts, Martha Will - 31
Presbytery - 4
    (Picture) - 6
Primitive Baptist - 4, 16

## -R-

Raley, Charles B. (Rev.) - 39-40
Revival - 4, 5, 8, 22, 23, 24, 20, 25-34, 36, 37, 40, 42, 47, 51, 53, 54
    Joint Revival - 55
Reynolds, Ann - 58
Richburg, David (Rev.) -42-43
    (Picture) - 42, 43
Richburg, David II -42
    (Picture) - 42
Richburg, Marica -42
    (Picture) - 42
Richburg, Mary -42
    (Picture) - 42
Roberts, Leon - 42
    (Picture) - 42
Rodgers, Wendall - 40, 42, 49, 71

## -S-

Sawyer, Claude -42, 70
Sawyer, Jimmy "James" D. (Chaplin). - 34, 37
Sawyer, John Ed. - 34
Sawyer, John (Rev.) - 49
Seay, J.A. (Rev.) -16
Seay, Murray L. (Rev.) -31
Scheffer, R. - 12
Sherrer, Anthony (Rev.) - 57
Shepherd, Silas (Rev.) - 39
Sims, Nathan (Rev.) - 53-56, 67
    (Picture) - 53
Stafford, Stacy (Rev,) - 54
Steiner, Rob "Wolf" -61, 73
Strength, Jim H. (Dr.) - 49
Stinson, Slade - 51
    (Picture) - 51
Strickland, Kyle A. - 57, 61, 73
Strozier, A.L. (Rev.) - 37
Stringfield, Craig (Rev.) - 53, 55
Smith, James Allen (Dr.) - 24, 33
Smith, Ronnie (Rev.) - 38

Steel, James Lee Roy (Dr.) - 32
Stewart, Anthony - 49

**South Carolina**
    Greenville - 42

Southeast Alabama Minister Conference - 48
Southern Baptist Convention - 71
Summer Youth Retreat - 55, 56
Sunday School - 22, 25, 27, 31, 46, 48, 72
    Sr. Ladies S.S. - 67
Sutherland, Billy (Rev.) - 63-64

## -T-

Talmadge, Joe (Dr.) - 49
Taylor, Dock - 5

**Texas**
    Brenham - 63-64
    Fort Worth - 31
    Montgomery Co. - 7
    Waco - 32

Thomas, C.S. - 18
Tindol, Billy - 49
Training Union - 25, 27
Traylor, Ted (Dr.) - 48

## -U-

U.S. Congressmen - 37
U.S. Navy - 37
U.S. Post Office - 10
U.S. Senators - 37

## -V-

Vacation Bible School (VBS) - 21, 22, 31, 37, 38, 55, 62, 72
    African American VBS - 31
    (Picture) - 38, 62-63

Valentine's Day Banquet - 61
Van Ministry - 48
Vice Moderator - 23
Volleyball Tournament - 40

## -W-

Walker, Sharon - 56, 68, 71
Walker, Stanley - 70
Wallace, J.N. - 14, 27, 29
    (Picture) - 27, 29
Wallace, J.N. (Mrs.) - 27
    (Picture) - 27
Walworth, Rodger (Dr.) - 55
Watson, Steven (Rev.) - 65
Watterson, Don (Dr.) - 45
Werlein, Christina - 64
Whitaker, Joshua (Rev.) - 68
Whitman, W.T. - 23
Williams, Danny (Rev.) - 56
Willingham, J. D. (Rev.) - 20
Willis, Tim - 54
Wilson, Josie - 5
Wilson, Mattie - 5
Winstead, Garry (Rev.) - 47
Winter Bible Study - 48
Wiregrass - 3
Wright, J.A. - 9, 14, 17
Woodall, J.B. (Dr.) - 18
Women's Missionary Union W.M.U. - 9, 16, 63, 66, 71-72

## -Y-

Y2K - 49
Y.M.C.A. - 40
Yarbrough, Hal - 52, 53
Young People Missionary - 16, 72-73
Youth Group - 16, 30, 59, 61-62, 72-73
    (Picture) - 59, 61-62
Youth Pastor - 57, 66
Youth Week - 30

Made in the USA
Columbia, SC
30 January 2024

cd2a4d1f-8b5e-4610-abb2-8258dbc9af58R01